Visions of Glory

Visions of Glory
Ezekiel

This inductive Bible study is designed for individual, small group, or classroom use. A leader's guide with full lesson plans and the answers to the Bible study questions is available from Regular Baptist Press. Order RBP0016 online at www.regularbaptistpress.org, e-mail orders@rbpstore.org, call toll-free 1-800-727-4440, or contact your distributor.

REGULAR BAPTIST PRESS
1300 North Meacham Road
Schaumburg, Illinois 60173-4806

The Doctrinal Basis of Our Curriculum

A more detailed statement with references is available upon request.

- The verbal, plenary inspiration of the Scriptures
- Only one true God
- The Trinity of the Godhead
- The Holy Spirit and His ministry
- The personality of Satan
- The Genesis account of creation
- Original sin and the fall of man
- The virgin birth of Christ
- Salvation through faith in the shed blood of Christ
- The bodily resurrection and priesthood of Christ
- Grace and the new birth
- Justification by faith
- Sanctification of the believer

- The security of the believer
- The church
- The ordinances of the local church: baptism by immersion and the Lord's Supper
- Biblical separation— ecclesiastical and personal
- Obedience to civil government
- The place of Israel
- The pretribulation rapture of the church
- The premillennial return of Christ
- The millennial reign of Christ
- Eternal glory in Heaven for the righteous
- Eternal torment in Hell for the wicked

VISIONS OF GLORY: EZEKIEL
Adult Bible Study Book
Vol. 58, No. 2
© 2009
Regular Baptist Press • Schaumburg, Illinois
www.regularbaptistpress.org • 1-800-727-4440
Printed in U.S.A.
All rights reserved
RBP0019 • ISBN: 978-1-60776-133-4

Contents

Preface

For many, the book of Ezekiel is like a 5,000-piece puzzle. They might have all the pieces, but they've lost the lid of the box, which contains the picture of the puzzle. As they look at the pieces, they are baffled. How will they ever put the puzzle together?

You will find that the book is simply designed. The prophet Ezekiel was ministering to the Jewish exiles in Babylon while God was chastising His sinning people. Ezekiel ministered at the same time that Daniel began to serve King Nebuchadnezzar in the courts of Babylon and that Jeremiah spoke God's word in Jerusalem.

The word that Ezekiel spoke had a context. Part of the context was God's covenant with His people; the other part was the over 800 years of Hebrew history between the giving of the covenant and Ezekiel's ministry. These contexts will help us understand Ezekiel. They're like the missing box lid of the puzzle.

The time you spend in Ezekiel will enrich your spiritual life. The book will deeply impress upon you the seriousness of sin and God's judgment on those who persist in it. You will grow in your knowledge of God's glory as you see both His justice and His amazing grace clearly illustrated.

Lord, I Want to Know You

Studying God's Word draws us closer to Him.

Overview of Ezekiel

"According as his divine power hath given unto us all things that pertain unto life and godliness, through the knowledge of him that hath called us to glory and virtue" (2 Peter 1:3).

This is going to hurt me more than it will hurt you."

"I am only doing this because I love you."

Perhaps your parents said these phrases or something similar to them right before they disciplined you. Maybe you have used these phrases too when you have had to discipline a child.

These phrases will probably be repeated in some form for generations to come, because children learn them during times of heightened awareness and then remember them when they go to discipline their children.

Disciplining should hurt both the person receiving it and the person giving it. As God dealt with His erring people, He disciplined them out of love as a means to restore them to Himself. He didn't enjoy disciplining them any more than a parent enjoys disciplining children.

Getting Started

1. When you were a child, how did you feel when your parents

repeatedly warned you about your behavior and then caught you in a major disobedience?

2. How do parents feel when they must discipline a disobedient child?

Searching the Scriptures

Knowing and obeying God was imperative for the Hebrews in Ezekiel's day, and it is still imperative for believers today. The book of Ezekiel reveals God to His people. In particular, the book covers three topics about God: God reveals Himself, God judges sin, and God restores His people.

3. What does it mean to "know" God?

4. Why do we need to know God fully?

God Revealed in His Word

Gaining a greater knowledge of our God should be a powerful motivation for studying Ezekiel. He reveals Himself in interesting ways through Ezekiel's messages.

5. Read Ezekiel 1:1–3. What do you learn about Ezekiel the man?

6. How did God reveal His word and will to Ezekiel?

The timing (the beginning of Ezekiel's priesthood), the place (in captivity in Babylon), and the means of God's revelation to Ezekiel (visions)—these three elements provide the keys to effectively study the book of Ezekiel.

As he began his book, Ezekiel left no room for questioning the source of his prophecy. In verse 1, Ezekiel unveiled his major theme: revealing God. In verse 3, he asserted that the hand of the Lord was upon him, and he revealed his authority to teach and preach. Ezekiel's words and actions resulted from God's work in his life. Ezekiel knew God personally.

7. How does personally knowing God affect you when you read the Bible, God's written revelation?

The Word of God is special revelation. It reveals God's person. The Word moves us beyond knowledge that God exists to knowledge of the God Who exists.

Now that the Scripture is complete, it is sufficient revelation for all the needs of our lives (2 Tim. 3:16, 17). We must simply obey the Word of God that we have received. We must go to the Word to learn about God.

God Revealed by His Word

The Bible is the written Word of God and the revelation of God. What does the Word—which reveals God—reveal *about* Him?

The Bible shows that God is the ruling God. When Ezekiel wrote that he was "among the captives [exiles] by the river of Chebar," he revealed how God was working out His plan to purify Israel. God's people should have been in God's land, enjoying God's blessing. Instead, they were out of God's land, under God's judgment. This fact is essential to understanding the book of Ezekiel. How could such judgment take place? To find the answer, we must think through some central Old Testament truths.

8. Read Genesis 12:1–3. Identify the three elements of God's covenant with Abraham.

The Old Testament details God's work with His people in light of the Abrahamic Covenant. In fact, His program here on earth focuses on the fulfillment of the promises made to Abraham.

The book of Deuteronomy is the covenant that God made with Abraham's descendants, the nation of Israel.

9. Read Deuteronomy 7:6–11. Identify Israel's responsibility toward that covenant.

If Israel didn't live up to her responsibility, God's plan also included the possibility of terrible chastisement and judgment.

10. Read Exodus 20:1–3. What is the first of the Ten Commandments?

11. Why would God give that particular command?

12. Why is idolatry, or the worship of anyone or anything other than God, an offense to God?

13. How do you react when someone disobeys you?

14. Skim through Deuteronomy 28:15–25, 32–37 and identify some of the things God said would happen if Israel disobeyed Him.

The first of the Ten Commandments tells of the uniqueness and singularity of God. He is the only God, and therefore He must be the sole object of worship (Deut. 5:6–8). Idolatry amounts to rejection of God. It allows another to be in His rightful place. For such foolish disobedience, God promised to chastise His people (Deut. 28:15–68).

The Bible also shows that God would graciously turn from judgment and restore His people when they repented. However, stiff-necked resistance to God would bring about the worst chastisement—captivity in a foreign land. The ten tribes that made up the Northern Kingdom of Israel had already been scattered in God's judgment (2 Kings 17:7–23).

15. If you had lived in the Southern Kingdom, would the captivity of the Northern Kingdom have taught you anything? If so, what? Why?

16. Why is it so hard for us to obey God's commands, especially when we see the consequences of others' disobedience?

The Southern Kingdom, Judah, had not learned from the chastisement of the Northern Kingdom. Their sins brought them to captivity too (2 Kings 25). Thus we find Ezekiel in exile among them in Babylon by the Chebar River.

The only God—Who has revealed Himself in His Word—had fulfilled His Word by judging His people. His judgment was in accord with His Word, yet He did not abandon His people. He ministered His Word to them through His prophet. The God Who judges is also the God Who longs to restore His people if only they will submit to Him.

17. Do you agree that God always punishes sin? Why or why not?

The Sin of Judah

Although God judges sin, He is gracious and gives repeated warnings before He judges. Ezekiel recounted God's gracious work with sinners. He both spoke and exemplified God's word. Ezekiel himself was actually one of the communication tools that God used to present His love and grace to needy sinners.

The truth that we worship a God Who is willing to judge sin is sobering. On the one hand, God's judgment calls lost sinners to repent. On the other, it calls God's people to purity (1 Peter 4:17).

For those who have trusted Christ for salvation, God's judgment does not carry the threat of Hell. The believer's sins have been fully dealt with at the cross (Rom. 8:1). However, believers may be chastised by God for sin.

18. Read Hebrews 12:5–15. Why does God chasten His children?

19. How should a believer respond to God's chastening?

20. What is the goal of God's chastening?

21. What profit comes from this loving chastening?

Ezekiel was a righteous man, but he still had to live through the judgment that God brought on the unbelieving nation. This judgment, though painful, drew him closer to God.

The Sin of the Nations

The nations around Israel knew about God because of their involvement with Israel. They should have submitted to Him, but they did not. Ezekiel preached God's plans for judgment on the nations, first on those closest to Judah and then on those at a distance.

In each case God revealed the nation's need to repent of specific sins. God knew the situation of each sinning group and called them to repentance based on their offenses.

Though sinners bear the responsibility for their behavior, Ezekiel revealed that the Devil is God's adversary and the moving force behind the nations who oppose God's plan. John recorded that "the whole world lieth in wickedness," or in the grip of the wicked one (1 John 5:19).

God Restores His People

Both the Northern Kingdom and the Southern Kingdom succumbed to wickedness. Judgment followed. But Isaiah, Jeremiah, and Ezekiel prophesied the promise of restoration based on God's unconditional covenant with Abraham. God will bring all the promises of the covenant to fulfillment in His way and in His time. Even though His people were in exile (1:1–3), He could present the promise of restoration to them.

When Israel comes to genuine spiritual life, she can be fully restored to the land and receive the promises of God's covenant. A rebuilt temple during Christ's Millennial Kingdom will provide a place for the people to offer memorial offerings to God. In this way they will celebrate and remember God's great work on their behalf.

Worship ought to be the result of a true knowledge of God. The "God-ward" focus of Israel's worship in the Millennium provides a thought-provoking example for the church. True worship turns attention from the individual and exults in God.

Ezekiel's writing is part of God's plan to thoroughly furnish us unto all good works (2 Tim. 3:17). However, we are God's church, not Israel, so we must apply Ezekiel in a way that is consistent with our dispensation.

We can identify a number of similarities between our situation and Ezekiel's. The descendants of Abraham, Isaac, and Jacob came to God by faith, just as we do. Their sins were washed away by the blood of Christ, just as ours are (Rom. 3:23–26). They lived with a goal of holiness and were sustained and guided by the Word of God. They enjoyed a rich spiritual life. In these and other ways, Israel's life parallels the church's life. However, similarity is not identity.

22. What are some obvious distinctions between Israel and the church?

The church is not Israel. It is made up of people living around the world from all nations and races. We do not share the genetic code of Abraham to tie us together. Instead, we are a part of the Body of Christ, related to the Head of the Body, Jesus Christ (Colossians 1:18–20).

The New Testament Scripture is our detailed plan for ministry in the Body while the Old Testament is both a guide and an encouragement. As we apply the book of Ezekiel to ourselves, we cannot join Israel in claiming the national promises, but we can grow in holiness.

We can learn the incomparability of God from the first three chapters, and God's judgment of sin should convict our hearts, identifying needs in our own lives. God's future restoration of Israel reveals that we have the opportunity of renewed fellowship with God on the personal level after we confess our sin.

Making It Personal

23. Will you commit to studying the book of Ezekiel regularly? If so, set an appointment and record it where you normally record your appointments.

24. Do you have any idols—things that replace God in your affections, time, spending, etc.? Confess your idolatry to God and ask Him to reveal Himself to you through Ezekiel in ways that will help you put Him first.

25. Memorize 2 Peter 1:3.

All the Equipment You'll Need

God prepares us thoroughly for the tasks He assigns to us.

Ezekiel 1—3

"And thou shalt speak my words unto them, whether they will hear, or whether they will forbear: for they are most rebellious" (Ezekiel 2:7).

Imagine a nurse is prepping you for an operation when you notice a maintenance cart with all kinds of tools on it being wheeled into the operating room. Curious, you ask your nurse what is going on. She tells you that your surgeon requested the tools for your operation. A moment later you see a surgical assistant carrying in a sledgehammer. You ask your nurse what it is for, and she tells you the anesthesiologist requested it. Most likely you would be looking for the nearest exit before your doctors came near you with their tools.

Have you ever stopped to think what "tools" a person would need to succeed as a prophet?

Getting Started

1. How would you respond if you were given a task but not the equipment or authority to accomplish it?

2. How would you respond if you had equipment but didn't know the task expected of you?

When God called Ezekiel to a difficult job, He provided the things—equipment, so to speak—that Ezekiel would need to carry out the job. And then God described the job.

Searching the Scriptures

The first three chapters of Ezekiel show how God equipped the prophet to do his assigned ministry. To encourage Ezekiel, God gave him a unique experience.

Sensory Overload

As God gave Ezekiel a special introduction to His calling in Ezekiel's life, Ezekiel experienced sensory overload.

3. Describe a time when you experienced sensory overload.

4. Read Ezekiel 1:4–28. What are the sights and sounds that catch your attention in this passage?

As Ezekiel tried to grasp all that he saw, he responded by falling on his face in worship.

5. What about God has recently filled you with wonder and caused you to worship Him?

Ezekiel 1 shows us at least two important attributes of God that can give us confidence as we serve Him.

6. What do you think the creature with the four faces revealed about God (Ezekiel 1:5–12)?

The curious creatures with four faces are a mystery to us. Chapter 10 implies that they were cherubim, which exist to serve God, carrying out His will in whatever manner He desires. Since the four creatures were joined to one another, their faces, totaling sixteen, looked in every direction simultaneously.

Because they faced in all directions at once and did not need to turn as they moved, there was no delay in carrying out God's will. Their motion was like a flash of lightning. Verse 12 says that the creatures moved under the direction of the spirit. Our God can accomplish anything He pleases immediately. Theologians use the term "omnipotence" to describe this attribute of God. The term means "all powerful." All that God does, He does effortlessly.

7. What do you think the wheels revealed about God (Ezekiel 1:15–18)?

This vision of the wheels seems to reveal that God is all-knowing. "Omniscience" is the theological term that describes this attribute. He knows all things, including what is possible and what is actual. His knowledge is not the result of a learning process, as ours is, but is immediate. The "wheel in the middle of a wheel" (v. 16) was full of eyes, and the rims were surrounded with eyes. The eyes depict God's knowledge of all things at all times and in all situations.

No turn of events takes God by surprise. Nothing is hidden from Him. Nothing prevents the accomplishment of His purpose.

Overwhelming Glory

Above the moving cherubim and wheels was a firmament, or canopy. The figure Ezekiel saw on the firmament was stationary.

8. All the activity below the firmament was directed by the figure above it (Ezekiel 1:26–28). What about God might that fact have revealed?

God is the sovereign ruler of the universe. He rules from above, and His thoughts and ways are different from and superior to ours (Isa. 55:9). So God is separate from us yet vitally involved with us and with all of His creation.

In a short time, God would reveal the sordid sins of the Children of Israel in all their grimy detail. Again and again, the prophet would face sin and its effects. In such a situation, it would have been easy to focus on the pervasive sin and to become discouraged. Ezekiel needed an understanding of the greatness of God to sustain him.

For effective service, we, too, must have God's character and mighty power impressed upon our minds. Because God is all-powerful, all-knowing, and above yet involved in our lives, we can confidently serve Him.

Rebellious Recipients of God's Word

In Ezekiel 2:1 God called Ezekiel "Son of man," which highlights his frail humanity. As Ezekiel humbly allowed God's Spirit to work through him, he fulfilled God's commission. As a "son of man," Ezekiel was dependent on God.

Like Ezekiel, the Children of Israel were frail humanity; but unlike him, they did not depend on God.

9. Read Ezekiel 2:1–8. How does this passage describe Israel?

Israel's sinful behavior was rooted in rebellion against God. God repeated the word "rebellious" often to underscore the prophet's task and to remind him of the daunting problem he would face.

Ezekiel's ministry was founded on the authority of God's Word (2:4). Even if the rebels chose not to listen to him, the prophet could not alter the message to suit the listeners. The problem was with the hearers, not with the message or the messenger. Whatever the response, the prophet was to speak the Word.

10. Describe a time when you or someone you knew obediently spoke God's Word but was rebuffed.

11. What is your responsibility when others reject God's Word?

12. Why must you be faithful to the Word of God?

Whether Israel responded or not, the people would realize "that there hath been a prophet among them" (v. 5). Ultimately, Ezekiel's ministry success would be measured by his faithfulness in proclaiming God's Word to the people.

Prophetic Preparation

Even though Ezekiel knew the standard for success, how would he accomplish the task? In his vision, Ezekiel received the remainder of the equipment he needed.

First, a hand presented him with the Word of God. As Ezekiel examined it, he noticed that the scroll was fully covered with "lamentations, and mourning, and woe" (Ezek. 2:10). Usually, only the inside of a scroll was used for writing, but this one had writing on the outside as well. This exceptional amount of revelation indicated the great extent of Israel's sin.

13. Read Ezekiel 2:10. What thought do you think went through Ezekiel's mind when he noticed the amount of writing on the scroll?

Next, God commanded Ezekiel to eat the scroll. The act of eating the scroll pictures Ezekiel's full acceptance of its message. It became a part of him.

14. Read Ezekiel 3:1–3. Since the scroll was filled with God's words about a sinful nation, how would you expect it to taste?

The Lord also prepared Ezekiel's attitude. The prophet's name means "God strengthens" or "God hardens." Israel's rejection of the prophet's word certainly would wear Ezekiel down over time. To protect him, God assured the prophet that He would make "thy face strong against their faces, and thy forehead strong against their foreheads" (3:8). Ezekiel became as sharp and as hard as flint (v. 9). Once again, God emphasized Ezekiel's responsibility to speak God's Word, no matter what response he received.

When the vision ended, God took Ezekiel back to the other exiles. He sat speechless, overcome by the revelation and the task (v. 15).

What preparation Ezekiel had received! First, he saw God Himself. Then, he internalized the Word. Through this, God fortified his outlook and gave him strength. Only one thing remained. He needed to know what to do.

Warning from the Watchman

15. Read Ezekiel 3:16, 17. What job did God give to Ezekiel?

In Old Testament times, a watchman stood on the city walls to warn against danger to the city. He was responsible to provide the people with advance warning of threats. If he did not warn, he would bear guilt.

16. Read Ezekiel 3:18–20. What did God hold Ezekiel responsible for: faithfulness in delivering the message or the success of the message? Explain.

Ezekiel was God's spiritual watchman, responsible to tell the people they could lose their lives for disobedience. If he failed to pass along

God's warning, God would hold him accountable.

Warning for the Watchman

Ezekiel was just as responsible to obey as the people were. If he failed to fulfill the watchman's role, he would fail as a prophet. The Lord delivered a dire warning to Ezekiel: failure on his part was tantamount to murder. This was a life-and-death matter. If those who were disobedient did not turn, they would die.

The disobedient would lose their lives—not their souls—for lack of a warning. The penalty for long-term idolatrous disobedience of the law was physical death. The prophet had the responsibility to warn those whose conduct was bringing them near death. Then it was up to each individual. Likewise today, every person will either pay the price of sin or reap the blessing of properly responding to God.

We must interpret Ezekiel 3:18–21 in its Biblical context. This warning does not address our responsibility to evangelize. The "loss of souls" in verses 18–20 refers to loss of physical life as a penalty for Israel's idolatry. It emphasizes the need to live a righteous life or face the consequences.

All people stand condemned, and all desperately need a Savior (John 3:18). We ought to declare their need for salvation, along with Christ's full provision for that need.

The fact that God removed disobedient Israelites from the earth by death may remind us of the chastisement that God inflicted on the Corinthians.

17. Read 1 Corinthians 11:27–30. What happened to some believers because they chose to continue in sin?

18. What is the application for us?

Waiting by the Watchman

As God's preparation of Ezekiel was ending, God once again showed Ezekiel His glory. The prophet's response was the same. No matter what equipping God provided for him or how thoroughly God explained Ezekiel's role, the prophet was merely a man. In the presence of the great God, Ezekiel fell on his face in worship.

19. Read Ezekiel 3:26, 27. What unique thing did God do to Ezekiel?

20. Why do you think He did that?

Ezekiel's mute condition lasted for over seven years, until the fall of the city of Jerusalem in 586 BC.

The prophet was then fully prepared for his ministry. He had seen God, had received God's Word, and knew exactly how he was supposed to minister. Next, he waited on God to show him the timing for his work.

Making It Personal

Ezekiel needed to see God in His glory and be strengthened with God-given resolve to face the task ahead.

21. Write out and meditate on three or four verses about God's glory that will help you face difficult times with faith in God instead of collapsing in defeat.

22. According to Psalm 119:103, God's Word is sweeter than honey. Are you getting a daily dose of sweetness? What will you do to add or increase your daily time in God's Word?

23. How does God expect you to be a watchman in your home, place of work, neighborhood, and church?

24. Write a prayer of commitment to rely on God to equip/prepare you to be the watchman He wants you to be.

25. Memorize Ezekiel 2:7.

Living Epistles

God uses His people to announce His judgment.

Ezekiel 4—7

"I will do unto them after their way, and according to their deserts will I judge them; and they shall know that I am the LORD" (Ezekiel 7:27b).

In the late nineteenth to early twentieth century lived a British lady who ministered in India. She used tea to stain her skin, wore saris, and thanked God for the brown eyes she had at one time despised. You may have recognized her; yes, Amy Carmichael. By changing her appearance, she did something that seemed strange to her fellow Britons, but she did it so she could minister more effectively to women and children in India.

In today's lesson, we'll learn how the prophet Ezekiel did some strange things for the sake of his ministry to the people of Israel.

Getting Started

1. Is there any shame in shaving one's head? Explain.

2. Would you be willing to shave your head as a vivid illustration of a Biblical truth?

3. Have you ever done something unusual so you could have a better opportunity to tell others about Christ? If so, what was it?

When God gave Ezekiel his assignment to be a watchman, Ezekiel had no idea of the strange—*really strange*—things God would tell him to do in order to show the people of Israel exactly why they suffered as they did.

Attack of the Toy Soldiers

Ezekiel used a sun-baked brick as the centerpiece of a long drama (Ezekiel 4:1). Much as a child would build a castle at the beach, he sculpted the siege of Jerusalem (vv. 2, 3). It was complete with "the camp against it" (the attacking army, v. 2) and all the siege works and ramps that would lead to the city's downfall. After Ezekiel built the model, God commanded him to lie on his side (v. 4). Ezekiel would thus "besiege" the city (vv. 2, 3).

Read Ezekiel 4:4–8.

4. Who was Ezekiel representing as he lay between the city and the army?

5. What did this signify?

Daniel 1:1–3 makes it clear that God was directly involved in the fall of Jerusalem, delivering the city into the hands of its enemies.

6. Why did God instruct Ezekiel to lie part of the time on his left side and part on his right (Ezekiel 4:4–6)?

Ezekiel lay on his left side for 390 days (vv. 4, 5). Each day represented one year of sin that God's people had committed. Then Ezekiel lay on his right side for forty days (v. 6), which may have represented Manassah's reign before he repented (2 Chronicles 33:13–16, 18).

As he lay, Ezekiel was bearing the iniquity of the house of Israel and Judah. In no sense was he a substitutionary offering for the sins of the people. He was a representative bearing testimony to their sin, not a substitute. Only the sacrifice of God's Son, Jesus Christ, can substitute for sins. He paid for sins when He died in place of sinners. Ezekiel's actions depicted Israel's sins, but couldn't remove them.

7. According to Ezekiel 4:9–12, what kind of diet was Ezekiel to observe?

Ezekiel's diet symbolized the way the people of Jerusalem would barely exist under siege conditions. Both grain and water would be scarce. In addition to this meager diet, God commanded Ezekiel to bake his bread over a fire made unclean by burning human dung. Use of animal dung was common in cooking food, but use of human dung was prohibited.

Ezekiel had been faithful to God. He had never eaten unclean food. So he sought a more appropriate fuel (v. 14). God graciously allowed him to use cow's dung (v. 15). The exiles, though, would eat the unclean food of the nation to which they would be taken (vv. 16, 17). A few, like Daniel, would choose to obey God no matter what their circumstances (Daniel 1:8).

It seems likely that Ezekiel's prophetic actions took place at set times of the day. Evidently, people would visit him to see his prophetic enactments. Ezekiel's actions, without spoken word, taught truth. His unwillingness to defile his food by baking it over human excrement honored God. As a prophet, he modeled God's activity in His people's lives.

8. Without doing strange things like those Ezekiel did, how can our lives illustrate God's work with mankind?

Hair Be Gone

The next strange thing God instructed Ezekiel to do was shave his head and beard, weigh the hair, and divide it into three groups (Ezekiel 5:1–4). This act signified humiliation or defilement. Ezekiel's humiliation therefore symbolized the humiliation of the nation: One third of the people would be burned when Jerusalem was burned after the siege (Ezekiel 5:2). Another third would be killed by the sword when the city fell (v. 2). Another third would be scattered to the wind in captivity (v. 2). But a remnant would be delivered (v. 3).

Judgment for Good Reasons

According to Ezekiel 5:5, God had placed Jerusalem as the focal point of His program on earth and had greatly blessed the city. Because Judah ignored God's Word and grace, judgment was on its way.

9. What did God explain in Ezekiel 5:9 about the coming judgments?

10. What were some of the judgments God would send upon Judah? Why did God send such harsh punishment?

11. According to Ezekiel 5:6 and 7, what terrible sins had the people committed that led to such harsh judgment?

The degree of the people's rebellion is amazing. They had actually and willfully exceeded their pagan neighbors in sinfulness. Though they possessed God's Word, they ignored it. By their actions, they opposed the truth.

12. Ezekiel 5:8 and 9 indicate another sin the people committed that led to such harsh judgment. What was it?

The first of the Ten Commandments proclaims the need to worship God alone. The word "abominations" in verse 9 refers to idolatry. The Israelites had first "demoted God" by making Him only one of many deities. Then they had turned their backs on Him and worshiped false gods.

God detests idols. They are nothing themselves (1 Corinthians 8:1–7). And He considers them abominable because they move the worshiper's focus from God. Idolatry is an attempt to shape God in one's own image. It reduces the God of the universe to a size that is manageable by humans.

13. Read Ezekiel 5:11 and name another sin committed by God's people.

The worship of idols offended God greatly. However, the Israelites had gone a step further, combining the worship of the one true God with the worship of false gods in the house of God. He demands that His people worship Him alone.

14. Ezekiel 6:8–10 identifies yet another sin that led to such harsh judgment. What was it?

The nation had broken her relationship with God for the supposed pleasure of a relationship with another. Israel, Ezekiel asserted, had a whorish heart (Ezekiel 6:9). The heart, as used in this passage, refers to the mind and the reasoning process. It's the seat of logical thinking. By deliberate choice, the Israelites had turned their hearts to another.

Only after judgment, when the passion of their adultery was cooled by the judgment of God, would they see the truth (vv. 8–10). When they did see the truth, they saw themselves from God's perspective.

15. In what ways do believers today commit the same sins?

16. Is God any less offended by these sins now than He was in Ezekiel's day?

17. What does the world think when they see believers committing these sins?

Results of Judgment

In Ezekiel 7:1–27, Ezekiel sketched the situation in a few words. The people had sown their wild oats, and there would be no crop failure. The judgment was as terrifying as it was complete.

18. Read Ezekiel 7:11–16, 21, and 22. What would happen to the people, economy, society, city, and property as a result of God's judgment?

19. Could similar judgment come upon believers today?

The Scripture teaches that sins are judged at the cross. Those who have trusted Christ are completely and eternally saved. Believers cannot lose their salvation or their standing before God. However, our righteous God is concerned that we develop a righteous life. In the case of Ananias and Sapphira (Acts 5) and the Corinthians who misused the Lord's Table (1 Corinthians 11:30), God's judgment was quite thorough. We must choose to live far from the sin that God exposes in His Word.

20. According to Ezekiel 6:7, 10, 13, and 14 and 7:4, 9, and 27, what was the only good outcome from the judgment on the Children of Israel?

21. Describe a time when God's chastisement of you caused you to know Him better.

God's wrath is purposeful. When Israel chose not to respond to God's Word or to His prophets, the Lord sent His wrath to allow the nation to know Him. Certainly, it is wiser to come to know God by obeying His Word.

Seven times Ezekiel spoke of God's desire that His people would know Him. The word used for "know" goes beyond a mere knowledge of the facts of God. It refers to a knowledge gained by personal experience. The warning is dire, though. If people do not choose to know God as Savior, they will know Him as Judge.

Israel should have been aware of this. The book of Exodus reveals that as God taught the Israelites in Egypt about Himself, He also taught the Egyptians. Israel learned the blessing of God's might while Egypt learned the cost of rebellion. The Egyptians came to know Him by experience, though they did not submit to His love. In Ezekiel's day, Israel was in a situation similar to Egypt's.

The Lord wishes the lost to learn of Him, and we are the letters, or living epistles like Ezekiel, whom He sends so unbelievers can know.

Making It Personal

22. Are you guilty of any of the sins committed by Israel? If so, are you willing to repent, confess, and forsake those sins? On a separate sheet of paper, write out a prayer. Sign and date it and place it in a safe place. Bring it out often to remind yourself of this decision.

23. Evaluate the way in which this past week you carried out your responsibilities as a watchman to warn sinners of coming judgment. Where would you put yourself on the line?

AWOL_____99.9% Faithful

24. What are some ways that you can live God's Word before unbelievers?

25. How well do you follow that up with a spoken witness?

26. Memorize Ezekiel 7:27b.

Lesson 4

Truth
and Consequences

We can't hide sin from God, so we can't avoid sin's consequences.

Ezekiel 8—11

"And I will give them one heart, and I will put a new spirit within you; and I will take the stony heart out of their flesh, and will give them an heart of flesh" (Ezekiel 11:19).

A little girl wanted to sneak up on her grandfather, so she approached him backwards. In her mind, if she couldn't see him, he couldn't see her. No doubt her grandfather chuckled as she "surprised" him.

The little girl's attempt at hiding is evidence of her immature way of thinking. We laugh at her silliness because we know that we must be out of sight to be truly hidden. However, we sometimes fail to remember that God sees everything. We are being just as silly as the little girl was when we think we can hide anything, particularly our sins, from God.

Getting Started

1. How do you feel when you think you have successfully hidden something?

2. Have you ever had a false sense of security?

3. Have you ever felt like you could hide something from God?

The Children of Israel thought they could hide their sins from God, but of course they could not. God made this clear to them through Ezekiel.

Searching the Scriptures

The fall of the Southern Kingdom did not take place with one decisive battle. Defeated Hebrews were taken to Babylon, but others remained in Judah.

The exiled elders of Judah were eager to learn of God's plan for them and their nation. Since Ezekiel could speak only when God specifically directed him to speak, the elders waited in his house, hoping to hear from the Lord. It was in that setting that "the hand of the Lord GOD fell" on Ezekiel (Ezekiel 8:1).

Ezekiel saw a vision. In it, he was lifted by the hair to travel back to Jerusalem (8:3, 4). In the temple he again saw God's glory. Against that backdrop, he saw the stark contrast of idolatry (v. 5). Ezekiel listed three specific sins that God would call to account.

Worshiping Idols

4. Read Ezekiel 8:5, 6. What was the first sin God would call to account?

5. How do you think God felt about the idolatry in His temple?

6. How do you feel when you have repeatedly told someone something and they willfully ignore you?

An "image of jealousy" (v. 5) was an idol that provoked God to jealousy. An idol is something worshiped in the place of God. God is God alone. Joining the worship of the Lord with the worship of an idol is blasphemous (impiously irreverent). There is only one God. There is no alternative.

The apostle Paul exposed the foolishness of idolatry when he asserted, "And [they] changed the glory of the incorruptible God into an image made like to corruptible man, and to birds, and fourfooted beasts, and creeping things" (Romans 1:23). When Israel turned her back on the truth of God's Word, she lost her concept of God.

Blaspheming God

The presence of an idol was not the worst that Ezekiel would see—just the most obvious.

Back in Judah, the Hebrew people continued their normal lives, including going to the temple with all of its rituals. As Ezekiel's vision progressed, he peeked through the hole he had made in the wall and saw a hidden door (Ezekiel 8:7–9). Behind that door, Ezekiel found the leaders of the nation involved in secret idolatry. While the idol in the temple was public, this sin was deeply hidden, as witnessed by the effort it took for Ezekiel to uncover it. However, it was not hidden from God.

7. Read Ezekiel 8:10–12. What two blasphemous (irreverent) ideas about God did the Jewish rulers have?

The Jewish rulers denied God's omniscience. They didn't know He was watching them. They thought He had left the country when they were defeated. They believed that if they were defeated in battle, then the victor's more powerful god had defeated their god.

Misdirected Worship

8. Read Ezekiel 8:13–17. What was the third sin God would call to account?

As Ezekiel watched in his vision, he saw the women of Israel worshiping Tammuz, an ancient Akkadian deity, who brought fertility to the land. He also saw twenty-five unidentified men worshiping the sun. Sun worship was forbidden by the covenant made with God (Deuteronomy 5:7, 8).

9. How would you expect God to respond to idolatry, blasphemy, and nature worship?

10. While Christ judged a believer's sins at Calvary, how does God respond to sin in a believer's life today? Does He see sin as trivial?

As a result of these sins, God would send judgment to match their actions (Ezekiel 8:18). Just as they had chosen to fill the land with violence, God would judge them violently. If this seems harsh to us, we must remember the patience and compassion of God. He had demonstrated His long-suffering for centuries.

Careful Assessment

Even as God promised judgment, He reminded Ezekiel of His mercy.

11. Read Ezekiel 9:1–6. How was God going to show mercy to the inhabitants of Jerusalem?

God would not judge the righteous ones who mourned over the nation's sins and repented. Repentance is a change of mind, a change from viewing ourselves from a human perspective to seeing ourselves as God sees us—sinners incapable of saving ourselves from sin. Jerusalem was filled with the unrepentant, and God's judgment was reserved for them.

12. If God's judgment is not random, then why do believers die along with unbelievers in natural disasters and man-caused tragedies?

Unprejudiced Judgment

The executions started where righteousness should have been most evident—among the religious leaders at the temple. Those who were serving in the temple should have been the most aware of God's uniqueness and sin's wrong. After the judgment at the temple, no one was left but the prophet (9:8). Ezekiel took no pride in his singular status. He compassionately cried to God for a reprieve.

Ezekiel's compassion was inappropriate. God's judgment was righteous for three reasons (v. 9). First, the sins of the nation had reached extraordinary proportions. Second, there was no regard for human life ("the land is full of blood"). Third, spiritual perversion filled the city. In answer to his plea for the people, Ezekiel was reminded of the degree of Israel's sin, of its manifestation in violence and injustice, and of Israel's blasphemy.

This judgment was what the people deserved. The words of the linen-clad scribe are a comfort, though. God's wrath did not fall on those who had been marked because of their righteousness (v. 11).

13. What have you learned about God's judgment from reading Ezekiel 9:1–11?

God's Glory Moves

14. Read Exodus 16:10; 40:34; 1 Kings 8:11. What did the physical manifestation of God's glory represent?

15. Read Ezekiel 9:3; 10:1–5. In Ezekiel's vision, what was happening to the glory of God?

16. Why was it happening? (See Deuteronomy 31:15–18 for help.)

The presence of God's glory was the proof of His relationship with Israel. It first came to them in the wilderness, manifested as a pillar of cloud and of fire (Exodus 16:10). When the Israelites built the tabernacle, the glory of the Lord filled the tabernacle (40:34). Still later, Solomon built the splendid temple of the Lord, and once again God's glory inhabited the innermost part of the temple, the holy of holies (1 Kings 8:11).

Now the opposite process was commencing (Ezekiel 9:2ff). The glory of God, the manifestation of His presence, moved from its historic location above the two cherubim of the mercy seat. As the judgment for sin began, the glory stood by the threshold.

When God commanded him, the man dressed in linen took coals of fire from below God's chariot (10:3). The coals may have symbolized judgment or cleansing.

God's glory left the temple and came to the chariot (v. 4ff). It was poised for departure, but in grace it delayed. The Lord's purpose for His people will be fulfilled in His time and in His way.

Moses had warned Israel of just such a possibility (Deuteronomy

31:15–18). In Ezekiel the terrible judgment was fulfilled. The glory left the temple threshold and went to the gate.

The spiritual dullness of the leaders of Israel becomes evident in Ezekiel 11:1–15. The Spirit identified them as "men that devise mischief, and give wicked counsel in this city" (11:2). Specifically, they assured the inhabitants of Jerusalem that God's judgment was not imminent. Jerusalem, they asserted, was like a cooking pot that protected the meat inside.

Rather than urging repentance, they urged the people to move ahead with life as usual. The Lord promised to bring them out of their secure cooking pot to fiery judgment. Though they thought they could dwell safely in the city, they would be judged at the borders of the land on their way to exile.

Through this most unpleasant means, God's purpose remained the same: He wants people to know Him. "Ye shall know that I am the LORD" (11:10, 12). If they will not know Him as the gracious Savior, they will yet know Him as the terrible Judge.

God's Grace Assures Restoration

Only God can free people from the consequences of sin. The promise of restoration to the Promised Land must have sounded sweet in the prophet's ears. God made a series of promises to restore His needy people.

First, He promised to be the sanctuary for the exiles in Babylon (v. 16). God Himself was their sanctuary now that the glory had departed from the temple. In one sense, they never lost the sanctuary—God moved with them!

Second, God promised to regather them to Israel (v. 17). In this, the darkest time of Israel's history, God's covenant remained firmly in place.

Third, God will bring spiritual life to His errant ones (v. 19). Jeremiah made the same promise to God's people in Jerusalem (Jeremiah 31—34). During the Tribulation, God's people will turn to Him for help, and He will give it!

In the meantime, though, unrepentant sinners will face God's judgment. They have earned it, and they will be paid the wages of their choice.

17. What will happen to Israel in the future?

18. With this, what will happen between God and Israel?

God's Glory Departs

With the words of verse 21 still echoing in his ears, Ezekiel saw the final departure of God's glory. Now nothing would prevent the full outflow of God's wrath upon His sinful people. When the nation's heart turns to God, He will save and restore the people. The glory will return in the Millennium (43:1, 2).

This ended the vision. The spirit then took Ezekiel back to Babylon to speak to the captives. He spoke everything that he had seen and heard. The coming judgment held great terror and little hope for the nation, which for the short term, was going to be destroyed. Only if the people would live righteously in their captivity would they enjoy the fellowship of God.

19. What does God require for anyone to have fellowship with Him?

20. How do people become righteous?

21. What does it take for believers today to enjoy fellowship with God?

Making It Personal

22. If you have not believed on Jesus and received Him as your personal Savior, will you do so right now?

23. If you are harboring sins, will you "sigh and cry" over them? Write a prayer, expressing to God your repentance.

24. If you previously repented and wrote a similar prayer, evaluate the level of your commitment to turn from that sin to God. Which of the following statements best describes you?

_____ I made an emotional response and haven't kept my commitment.

_____ I have been trying and failing to keep my commitment. I probably need counsel from a victorious Christian.

_____ I am, by the grace of God, sticking to my commitment— to Him be all the glory!

Now what will you do?

25. Memorize Ezekiel 11:19.

Enough Is Enough!

*God holds spiritual leaders accountable
for their leadership.*

Ezekiel 12—14

**"Therefore say unto them, Thus saith the Lord
GOD; There shall none of my words be prolonged
any more, but the word which I have spoken
shall be done, saith the Lord GOD" (Ezekiel
12:28).**

E nough is enough!" This is a strange saying, but we know
what it means. We say it when we become exasperated
with someone or something. Perhaps you are a mother who has said it
to your children after they refuse to listen to your repeated demands that
they stop bickering. Or perhaps you have said it when a neighbor keeps
annoying you with his loud garage band.

In today's lesson, we might imagine the Lord saying these words
to Judah. He wanted the people to scrutinize their lives carefully and
change their outlook completely.

Getting Started

1. Describe a time when you said, "Enough is enough!"

2. What was the outcome of the circumstances?

3. When have you regretted saying the phrase?

Searching the Scriptures

In Ezekiel 12—14, Ezekiel cited three elements that opposed God's work: rationalization, religion that denied God's Word, and idols in the heart. Then he told the people they must embrace two truths that would set them free: God fulfills His Word and He demands a repentant, obedient lifestyle.

Dramatizing God's Word

"The word of the LORD also came unto me" in Ezekiel 12:1 signals a new series of messages. In His grace, God provided two more dramatic presentations by Ezekiel.

4. Why do you think God combined drama with the spoken word?

Ezekiel brought out a few belongings and packed them in the sight of his neighbors (12:3, 4). Next he dug through the wall of his house (v. 5). Since the house was made of sun-dried bricks, the prophet could make a hole large enough for himself and his bag to pass. At evening, he climbed through the hole and covered his face with some sort of mask or cloth (vv. 6, 7).

The people watched and evidently asked questions, but Ezekiel was still unable to speak. The Lord did not open the prophet's mouth until the following morning (v. 8). The message was simple: more captives were coming, including a prince who would try to escape through the city wall (vv. 9–12). The armies of King Nebuchadnezzar ended his escape attempt in a most terrible way (vv. 13–16).

As God judged, His people would learn the hard way that He is the Lord. *He* was responsible for Babylon's judgment on Jerusalem (v. 13). *He* scattered Zedekiah's bodyguard and the captives. The few who were spared judgment were given captivity as an opportunity to repent.

5. Read Ezekiel 12:15. What statement of God's intent for the people is restated here?

6. What did God mean when He said that?

7. What has God done in your life recently to help you know Him better?

The second drama was a pantomime of fear (vv. 17–20). As Ezekiel ate, he pretended that he was terrified. His trembling and shuddering modeled the terror of Nebuchadnezzar's captives after the sacking of Jerusalem. Nebuchadnezzar would destroy all that they had known. Then the hostages would begin the long walk to captivity. All their emotions would be affected.

8. How does Ezekiel 12:17–20 demonstrate the fulfillment of God's Word?

9. In what ways do believers today doubt God's Word?

10. Is there any reason to mistrust what God has said?

Again God's goal in judgment was instructive: He wanted His people to know Him.

The Timing of God's Word

Though many had prophesied judgment, years had passed. There was even a proverb that said, "The days are prolonged, and every vision faileth" (v. 22). The people doubted that God's judgment would ever come. Judah should have seen this delay as proof of God's long-suffering and grace. Instead, they concluded that since judgment had not yet come, it might not happen at all. As they had with the prophets of old, the rationalizers of Judah ignored Ezekiel's word (v. 24).

11. Describe people's attitudes toward sin today.

12. What are some ways people rationalize their sin?

13. Do people seem to "connect" God's judgment with their sin? Why?

God's Word always comes to pass. God's timing depends on His purposes.

Identification of the Fools

While Ezekiel 12 speaks against the citizens of Judah who rational-ized away the fulfillment of God's Word, chapter 13 attacks the false prophets who encouraged their foolishness.

14. Read Psalms 14:1; 74:18; Ezekiel 13:3. What term does God ap-ply to people who lack spiritual discernment?

Ezekiel bluntly exposed the true nature of these religious leaders: they were fools (Ezekiel 13:3). This word refers to a lack of spiritual dis-cernment, not to a lack of mental ability.

The prophets relied on their own hearts (13:2) and spirits (v. 3). They delivered their own ideas, presenting those ideas as if God had spoken. They passed off their thoughts as God's thoughts and their feel-ings as God's feelings. They "proved" their statements through pagan divination (v. 9). Such foolishness may make a great outer show, but it does not result in God's Word.

The false prophets spoke in the name of God. Their message gave the illusion of comfort but offered no real help. The citizens of Judah did not want to hear from Ezekiel that God had ordained judgment against them.

The Lord characterized these prophets as "foxes in the deserts" (v. 4). As foxes, or jackals, play among the deserted ruins left by con-quering armies, and feed on the corpses of the fallen, so Judah's false prophets offered nothing beneficial.

In contrast, a true prophet would work to repair the broken wall to keep the foxes out. Ezekiel made the people uncomfortable as he exposed their sinful, idolatrous hearts. The false prophets made people comfortable, although they were, in fact, in danger of God's wrath.

Judgment on the Fools

Judah's false spiritual leaders led the people astray, promising peace when God had promised judgment. Ezekiel condemned women as well as men (vv. 17, 18).

The prophetesses made a great show of religion, but they hid the truth. They hunted people as one would hunt a bird (vv. 19, 20). They, too, would share in God's judgment.

The false prophets lulled sinners to spiritual lethargy through their deceiving words. Instead of calling the people to repentance, they promised life to the wicked, when the wages of sin is death.

In addition, they brought grief to the righteous. As the righteous tried to live according to God's Word, the message of these "professional prophets" discouraged them. Since the false prophets did not use the Word of God as their standard, they introduced another standard: their own thoughts.

15. Why do people, especially those who claim to be Christians, fall for leaders who are "foxes in the deserts" and their messages?

The fact that the false prophets spoke a message satisfying to hear did not make them speakers of truth. Lies spoken pleasingly are still lies. When God's Word comes to pass, as it surely will, it will be evident that God is the Lord.

The Command

As the elders of Israel sat before the prophet, they appeared to be upstanding citizens who sought God's direction. However, as God exposed their thoughts, Ezekiel learned that the elders were anything but righteous. They had idols in their hearts that kept them from worshiping the only God. The sin of the leaders was also present in the nation at large (14:1–4).

Some limit "idolatry" to participating in worship of a false god. First and foremost, though, idolatry is a matter of the heart (v. 5). Before the body ever bows to a statue, the heart submits to it. God demands wholehearted obedience. When the heart exalts anything except God, idolatry has set in.

16. Read Ezekiel 14:6. What was God's message to these idol worshipers?

17. If you had heard this message as often as the people in Judah had heard it, how would you have responded?

18. Is that how you respond to the conviction of the Holy Spirit in your heart?

God has a message for idolaters: repent! Remember that repentance is a redirecting of one's thoughts, a change of heart. Repentance involves more than thinking about something different. It is actually thinking in a new way, based on a new standard of truth.

The sure mark of repentance, according to 14:6, is a change of behavior. Ezekiel called the people to turn their backs on their idols and renounce their sinful idolatry. They would show their repentant hearts both physically and orally.

God also promised judgment on the false prophets who, by their pronouncements, supported the people's idolatry. When Babylon finally took the city of Jerusalem, these liars would die. Once again, the Lord reminded them of His purpose in judgment (v. 11): He is not vindictive; He desires a relationship based on a true understanding of His deity. Those who know God find satisfaction in Him. Ezekiel taught that idolatry does great damage, separating people from the one and only God and making truth inaccessible. It is a sin worthy of judgment.

The Consequence

When idolatry reached the level it had in Judah, judgment was inevitable. Once again, "the word of the LORD came" to Ezekiel. Four terrible judgments (famine, wild beasts, sword, and plague) would devastate the nation (vv. 17, 19–21). Was there any way to avert God's judgment? Perhaps if extraordinarily spiritual men were in Jerusalem, the judgment would be suspended. The prophet suggested three such men.

19. Read Ezekiel 14:14. Which three righteous men did Ezekiel cite as examples?

20. How did these men exemplify righteousness? See Genesis 6:9; Job 1:8; and Daniel 1:8.

We might think that the presence of three men of exemplary godliness would surely avert God's judgment. But the Lord made it clear that He would still punish. Had the three righteous men been in Judah, they would have been delivered (Ezekiel 14:14), but their righteousness could not have delivered others (14:16). Only personal righteousness can deliver from judgment.

After God judged the city, the newest group of exiles would end up in Babylon (vv. 22, 23).

21. Read Ezekiel 14:22, 23. How would the new remnant from Jerusalem behave in Babylon?

The behavior of the remnant from Jerusalem would comfort Ezekiel as he observed it. Their behavior would show that God's punishment was just.

Making It Personal

Ezekiel 12—14 demonstrates the importance of having godly spiritual leaders who will proclaim God's Word accurately and speak honestly about our sins.

22. What criteria should you use to evaluate potential spiritual leaders (Bible teachers/preachers; writers; Bible study leaders)?

If you are a spiritual leader in your home or church, you have a great responsibility. You are also a target for Satan, who would love to bring you down, since you would bring others with you.

23. Ask God to keep you from the sins like those in Judah as they might be manifested in a twenty-first century Christian.

24. Memorize Ezekiel 12:28.

Lesson 6

Six Sour Grapes

Sin produces unpleasant, undesirable fruit.

Ezekiel 16—18

"Behold, all souls are mine; as the soul of the father, so also the soul of the son is mine: the soul that sinneth, it shall die" (Ezekiel 18:4).

During times of economic downturn, people learn valuable lessons from the misfortunes of others. Those who have jobs learn from the those who have lost theirs, and many seek income protection insurance. Individuals can use an income protection plan to replace their incomes if they lose their jobs, and businesses can use it to protect against an unexpected decline in revenues. It's not surprising, then, that while sales of other kinds of insurance plans fall off in a down economy, sales of income protection plans rise.

If we have our druthers, we would probably prefer to learn from others' misfortunes and mistakes than from our own. But human nature is so twisted that sometimes people prefer to learn their lessons the hard way. This week's study in Ezekiel challenges us to learn them the easy way—from God and from others.

Getting Started

1. Describe a time when you learned by painful experience to avoid something (e.g., got burned, learned to avoid a hot stove).

2. List some things that you avoid because of other people's experiences or teaching (e.g., avoid snakes, learned from those who have been bitten; avoid evildoers, learned from the Bible, parents, etc.).

3. Which is the better way to learn about sin: from God or from your own experiences?

Searching the Scriptures

In Ezekiel 16—18, Ezekiel described the Israelites to a T. If we are wise, we will study this passage for the purpose of gaining wisdom.

Self-sufficient

God made it clear to the people of Israel that their beginning was one of humility and dependence on Him. He had made them great and famous. But in Ezekiel 16:15a He indicted Israel for self-sufficiency: "But thou didst trust in thine own beauty." She had forgotten her roots. All that she was and had, had come directly from the work of God. These humbling truths were part of God's covenant with the nation. According to Deuteronomy 7:8–11, God chose Israel because He loved her. She had no redeeming qualities to merit His love.

4. When are you most prone to become self-sufficient instead of being reliant on God?

Moses warned Israel of the danger that she would forget God after she began to enjoy the Promised Land. In the wilderness, Israel depended on God for everything at every moment. His pillar of cloud sheltered her by day, and His pillar of fire sheltered her at night. He provided manna and water.

5. According to Deuteronomy 6:10 and 11, what did God predict would happen when the Israelites inhabited the Promised Land?

6. Read Deuteronomy 6:12. What attitude could this lead to?

7. What picture does God use in Ezekiel 16:1–5 to describe Israel's roots?

8. Read Ezekiel 16:6–14. What two words would you use to describe God's actions on behalf of Israel?

To remind the Hebrews of their humble beginnings, Ezekiel described Israel as an unwanted and abandoned child (Ezekiel 16:4). The Lord found the child and met every need for her protection and growth. Continuing the analogy, the Lord clothed Israel and entered into a covenant with her. He enriched her (v. 10) and made her famous. He exalted her among the nations and gave her political leadership in the Near East.

9. While the church is different from Israel, in what ways does God treat believing sinners similarly to how He treated Israel in her infant state?

Rather than give thanks, Israel came to a deluded conclusion. The people began to believe they had achieved their position and glory through their own capabilities. They forgot that God's power had achieved it all.

Self-sufficiency is a terminal disease. It is one thing to take full advantage of the gifts that God gives. It is another to view those gifts as though we were the source of them.

10. In what ways do Christians demonstrate self-sufficiency?

Fallen human beings always struggle with God's grace. If Heaven cost only fifty cents, practically everyone would go there. In that way, they could do something to earn salvation. The fact that God's work is by grace frustrates sinful people. We want to do something to participate in God's saving work. However, grace has made that unnecessary and impossible.

The beginning of victory over sin is daily humility before God. Paul asserted, "But by the grace of God I am what I am: and his grace which was bestowed upon me was not in vain; but I laboured more abundantly than they all: yet not I, but the grace of God which was with me" (1 Corinthians 15:10).

Unfaithful

As Ezekiel continued his description of sinful Israel, he pointed out the nation's unfaithfulness.

11. Hosea 1:2 and 3 record the kind of wife God told Hosea to marry as a picture of Himself and Israel. What was she to be like?

Hosea's wife, Gomer, committed adultery against Hosea. The Bible often uses sexual immorality to picture spiritual unfaithfulness. In any age and in any place, an adulterer is unfaithful in an attempt to satisfy a sinful desire.

12. Read Hosea 2:4 and 5. Above and beyond her adultery, what did Gomer—and Israel—do?

Adultery is an ugly type of unfaithfulness, but prostitution takes unfaithfulness a step farther. Prostitution reduces the unfaithfulness to an economic choice.

God promised to meet Israel's needs as a nation. This promise was inclusive whether the needs were economic, political, social, or religious (Deuteronomy 28:1–14). Instead of trusting in the Lord, Israel made alliances with other nations. As the people of Israel began to interact with other nations, they adopted foreign customs including the worship of foreign gods.

Israel's spiritual prostitution was compounded by her use of God's gracious provision to entice others into relationships with her (Ezekiel 16:34). Her wealth had come as a gift from God, so this was a great perversion of the gift. In a downward spiral, this adulterous involvement with other nations introduced more idolatry into Israel.

Weakhearted

Wrong behavior is the most obvious evidence of sin. However, sin affects humanity at a deeper level than only behavior. Sin affects the deepest center of our being. "How weak is thine heart," the Lord told His people (Ezekiel 16:30). God was telling them they were spineless.

13. What are some synonyms for "spineless"?

The people had weak, untrustworthy hearts. Ezekiel was not referring to the physical heart, but to the mind and reasoning capacity. Just as the physical heart is the core of the body, so the functions of the mind control one's whole person.

14. What does Proverbs 28:26 say about trusting your heart?

We must admit that our problem with sin is "won't," not "can't." As believers, we can say no to temptation. In other words, by the power of the indwelling Spirit, through the Word of God, our minds can come into submission to God (Romans 12:1, 2).

Trust in God combined with His Word will renew the mind. We believers are not helpless victims but victors in Christ. We serve the God Who said in 1 Corinthians 10:13, "There hath no temptation taken you but such as is common to man: but God is faithful, who will not suffer you to be tempted above that ye are able; but will with the temptation also make a way to escape, that ye may be able to bear it." In this confidence, we must study the Bible to renew our thinking. We must choose the truth, as God has commanded us to do. In Christ, we are no longer spineless to do good.

Promiscuous

The Hebrew people were guilty of not only spiritual adultery and prostitution, but also of spiritual promiscuity. This word refers to someone who is "deficient in discrimination and discernment; unrestrained." It actually has a wider frame of reference than sexual immorality, though it is most often applied to such sins. The term "whoredoms" in Ezekiel 16:34 refers to the attitude that leads to the act.

15. Read Ezekiel 16:33 and 34. What did Israel do that even a prostitute wouldn't do?

Israel's action shows a wholesale lack of discrimination; it was completely unrestrained, almost desperate. Here we see the effect of idolatry. All moorings in righteousness were gone. Righteousness requires the standards of God's Word. Sin destroys those standards.

Snared

A snare is a hidden trap.

16. Have you ever caught anything in a snare?

17. How does it work?

The one who falls into a snare is surprised because he was not ready for a trap. In this context, King Zedekiah of Judah fell into the Lord's snare (Ezekiel 17:20). As a result, the king would be taken to Babylon as a captive. Sadly, Zedekiah's own foolishness led him into the snare. That is the effect of sin.

As Zedekiah tried to escape the siege of the city, his enemies caught him. Though he timed his escape for the dark of night and broke through the city wall in an unexpected place, it was to no avail. God had decreed that Zedekiah's enemies would capture him.

18. Read 2 Kings 25:1–7. What horrible things happened to Zedekiah after his enemies captured him?

Zedekiah had access to God's Word. In Deuteronomy 17:14–20, God specifically directed the kings of Israel and made promises to them. One of those promises was a long and secure reign (v. 20). The cost of God's guidance and protection was obedience. Zedekiah chose not to obey, and he paid a high price.

When an individual ignores God's Word, there is a price to pay. That price should come as no surprise, given the clarity of God's Word. We must choose to study and obey the Word of God. If we choose differently, our sins will lead us into a trap.

19. How sure are you that sin leads to a trap?

20. On what do you base your answer?

Held Responsible

We bear the blame for our own sins. In Ezekiel 18:2, the prophet quoted a popular saying of his day: "The fathers have eaten sour grapes, and the children's teeth are set on edge." It means that parents are to blame for the trouble their children experience. But Ezekiel told the people they were wrong. God assigns individual guilt for individual sin. They couldn't point their fingers at their parents. They were responsible for their own sins.

The people needed to point their fingers at their own hearts. Their parents were guilty, but each person was responsible for his own sin.

21. What are some other modern deceptions concerning sin?

Making It Personal

22. What are you doing daily to help yourself choose obedience and victory?

23. If you think obedience is too high a price, think again. You will pay a much higher price for holding on to your sin. Are you cuddling a self-sufficient attitude, spiritual adultery or promiscuity, or a weak heart? Confess and repent!

24. Memorize Ezekiel 18:4.

Lesson 7

The Loser's Share

Rebels against God lose in every way.

Ezekiel 20—24

"I the LORD have spoken it: it shall come to pass, and I will do it; I will not go back, neither will I spare, neither will I repent; according to thy ways, and according to thy doings, shall they judge thee, saith the Lord GOD" (Ezekiel 24:14).

Leave it to Americans to make winners out of losers. In 2004 a TV show called *The Biggest Loser* aired in the U.S. In subsequent years, the United Kingdom, Australia, Germany, Hungary, and India aired their own versions, as have Israel, the Middle East, Mexico, Netherlands, and South Africa. This weight-loss reality drama features celebrity fitness trainers who join with top health experts to help overweight contestants transform their bodies, health, and lives. The winner receives a cash prize in addition to all the benefits of being fit and trim.

While the show is "reality" because the contestants and the weight loss are real, the true reality is that no one wants to be considered a loser. No one wants a loser's life. No one wants to end a loser.

In our study of Ezekiel 20—24, we'll discover what causes a nation or an individual to be the bad kind of "loser."

Getting Started

1. What are some consequences of rebellion?

2. Describe a time when you rebelled as a child.

3. What was the consequence?

Searching the Scriptures

In Ezekiel 20—24, the Lord condemned the rebellion of Israel no less than five times. Rebellion makes a person a real loser. consider these four aftereffects of humiliation: humiliation, corruption, spiritual adultery, and emotional numbness.

We Don't Want To!

Over and over again, the people of Israel seemed to tell God, "We don't want to obey and serve You." Nevertheless, the people liked to put on a good show of interest in the Lord and His ways. So in August 591 BC, the elders came to Ezekiel "to inquire of the LORD." We do not know what their question was, but the answer was certainly clear. "Cause them to know the abominations of their fathers" (Ezekiel 20:4).

4. Read Ezekiel 20:8–12. How did the people rebel; how did God respond; and what was the purpose of His response?

5. Read verses 13–20. How did the people rebel; how did God respond; and what was the purpose of His response?

6. Read verses 21–28. How did the people rebel; how did God respond; and what was the purpose of His response?

This is the history of Israel's rebellion. Ezekiel's generation knew the history summarized in Ezekiel 20:1–29. They had seen its consequences, yet they persisted in similar rebellion.

Just like Mom and Dad

The Children of Israel in Ezekiel's day committed abominations just as their parents had (Ezekiel 20:30). They even sacrificed their children to idols (v. 31). Israel's sin had not changed; neither had God's purpose to redeem Israel. We see the depth of His grace as He promised to "plead with [them] face to face" (v. 35). He will return the people of Israel to their land (vv. 41, 42); He will do it for the sake of His name (v. 44). God's covenant with Abraham will be fulfilled. God has given His Word, and He will keep it! The future holds the completion of the covenant.

However, the future fulfillment of the covenant would not prevent God's judgment in the present. Once again, God commanded Ezekiel to communicate His word through dramatic performance (21:1–17).

For his first performance, Ezekiel was to sigh or groan (vv. 1–7).

7. What is the significance of a deep sigh or multiple sighs?

If people asked about his sighing, Ezekiel could tell them about the judgment that God was unleashing against the nation. When the judgment neared, the people would respond just as he had been acting.

Next Ezekiel sang to the people (vv. 8–17). His poem was about a sharpened sword. God would use the sword as the method of judgment against the sinful people and princes of Judah (v. 12). The slaughter would be great.

Ezekiel's third dramatic act required him to draw a map of the region from Babylon to Judah (vv. 18–24). The road from Babylon to Israel would end with a fork in the road. One side of the fork led to Judah and the other side to Ammon.

Ezekiel prophesied that the king of Babylon would stop at such a fork in the road and use divination to determine which way to go (21:21). He would be directed to Jerusalem. Unknown to Nebuchadnezzar, the Lord's hand of judgment was behind his choice. God had determined to immediately judge Judah for sin and temporarily delay the judgment of Ammon.

Once again, God's word of judgment concluded with a word of hope. "I will overturn, overturn, overturn, it: and it shall be no more, until he come whose right it is; and I will give it him" (v. 27).

8. In Ezekiel 21:27, to whom does the description "whose right it is" refer? (See Luke 1:31–33.)

9. What will happen when that person comes?

10. How should this truth have affected Israel?

When Jacob blessed his sons, he promised the coming of Messiah, Whose future rule will be marked with righteousness (Genesis 49:10). However, that future hope would not stop the judgment of Judah. She had rebelled against God in spite of His Word and His grace. The people would face the consequences of their actions.

Humiliation

As the consequence of Israel's rebellion, God had "made [the people] a reproach unto the heathen, and a mocking to all countries" (Ezekiel 22:4). They had become the laughingstock of the ancient Near East.

11. What sins are listed in Ezekiel 22:3–12?

Until judgment came, it seemed that the Hebrews were getting away with it all. But God would break their power as a nation and disperse them through other nations (v. 15), where they would live out their lives.

12. Would countries today be humiliated by the same laundry list of sins as found in Ezekiel 22? Explain.

Ezekiel used the example of a smelting furnace to depict God's judgment. "The house of Israel is to me become dross," God proclaimed (v. 18). The heat of His anger would be like the heat of a furnace that can melt metal. The Lord promised to pour out His fury. The people were proudly rebelling, living as though their actions had no consequences. So they would be wholly humiliated in front of the pagan nations around them.

Corruption

The second consequence of Judah's rebellion was corruption (22:23–31). Since the Hebrews were not moored to the absolutes of God's Word, every person followed his own corrupt desires. The leaders were especially at fault. They should have helped the people follow God. Instead, they led the way in sin.

13. How could a child of God in any age discern whether a prophet or a preacher/teacher is from God and telling the truth?

Since God's Word was not yet complete, God used prophets to bring His message to the people. When a prophet said, "Thus saith the Lord," he wielded great influence over the people. False prophets took advantage of the role of the prophet in Israel. If the people did not compare the prophet's word to Scripture, the lie of a false prophet would lead them astray. The false prophets counted on the people's trust, and then they took advantage of it.

The priests (22:26) should have taught the people God's Word. Instead, they ignored its most basic precept: holiness. They did not keep the Sabbath. The political leaders (v. 27) used their office to amass personal gain at the expense of others' lives. The false prophets (v. 28) helped both the priests and the political leaders commit their sins with impunity.

With such poor examples to follow, the people of the land committed the same types of sins. They abused some, took advantage of others, and lived out the example of their leaders.

14. What should a believer do about a false or godless preacher/teacher?

In Israel's youth, Moses "stood . . . in the breach" to pray for the people and to lead them to righteousness (Psalm 106:23). At this point in the degeneration of the nation, though, God could find no one to "stand in the gap" (Ezekiel 22:30). So, regardless of who did the rebelling—religious leaders, political leaders, or the people themselves—rebellion inevitably bore its rotten fruit. The people would face judgment.

Spiritual Adultery

Chapter 23 describes a third effect of rebellion. God desired for Israel to be His wife (Ezekiel 16:8). She rebelled against Him, establishing relationships with other nations. Though the Lord was her protection, she allied herself with the political powers of her day. This was spiritual adultery.

At any time of life, we may turn our backs on God's specific words and commit spiritual adultery. In Israel's case, the people tried to be a nation like all the other nations instead of a holy nation before the Lord.

15. Tell of a time when you needed to accomplish a pleasant goal but others did not cooperate.

16. What steps did you have to take to get their cooperation?

17. In what ways do we believers fight what is best for us?

God wanted His people to know Him. If judgment was the only means to accomplish that goal, He would judge them so they could know Him.

Emotional Numbness

The fourth effect of rebellion is numbness. Ultimately, rebellion brings such a devastating judgment that emotional overload sets in.

Chapter 24 is a separate oracle, or authoritative message, from the preceding section, but it still deals with the effects of rebellion. The message was given on the day that Nebuchadnezzar's armies began the final siege of Jerusalem in 598 BC (v. 2).

The first section of the chapter summarizes the sins for which Judah was judged and shows the nature of the judgment (vv. 1–14). The city was a cooking pot (v. 3) with the fire of God's judgment burning under it. The judgment was intense (v. 10). The pot boiled dry and the food was ruined, sticking to the sides of the pot.

18. Other than cooking, what's a reason for boiling something?

The fire of God's judgment would heat the pot to glowing in order to purify away the "scum," or impurity—but in vain. Though the judgment might be terrifying, God would see it through to the end. Jerusalem would receive what she deserved.

After describing the judgment, the Lord caused Ezekiel to be a sign to the exiles one more time (vv. 15–27). Ezekiel's wife would suddenly die, but he could not take up the usual practices of mourning (v. 16). God permitted him only to groan silently. In just a few hours, the prophet's life changed dramatically. Yet he obeyed the Lord and "did in the morning as I was commanded" (v. 18).

19. Describe a time when you were too stunned to show emotion.

Ezekiel's bizarre response to his wife's death brought questions from his incredulous countrymen (v. 19). His explanation was as unsettling as his actions. He was modeling what they would do when the judgment came (vv. 21–24). The suddenness and violence of the judgment would stress their emotions. They would become unable to express the feelings that Ezekiel was suppressing. Nebuchadnezzar would destroy the temple and even kill young children.

The next group of captives to come to Babylon would bear the news of Jerusalem's destruction (Ezekiel 25:25–27). On that day, Ezekiel's ministry style would change. Once again, he could speak at will instead of waiting for a revelation. Vindicated by the fulfillment of his words, Ezekiel, the sign from the Lord, would testify for Him.

Making It Personal

20. Do you condone or overlook the sins in our country that are similar to Judah's sins? Prayerfully evaluate these sins in light of Ezekiel 20—24.

21. What are the symptoms of a rebellious heart? How do you know if you are rebellious?

22. Memorize Ezekiel 24:14.

Who's behind the Sins of the Nations?

Satan motivates rebellions against God.

Ezekiel 25—28

"Submit yourselves therefore to God. Resist the devil, and he will flee from you" (James 4:7).

Hatred of Israel by nations today is as real as it was in Ezekiel's day. Iran is probably the leader in speaking out against Israel. Mahmoud Ahmadinejad, Iran's president, even called for the extinction of Israel.

In Ezekiel's day, the nations that opposed Israel included Ammon, Moab, and Edom. Cities such as Tyre and Sidon also did their share to trouble the Israelites. God promised vengeance on those nations and His words did not fail.

Getting Started

1. What do you think motivates people like Mahmoud Ahmadinejad to be so hateful of Israel today?

2. What part do you think Satan plays in hatred of Israel?

Searching the Scriptures

In chapters 1—24, Ezekiel brought attention to the sins of Judah. He identified them so thoroughly that we might wonder if any other nation had a problem with sin. If God's own people could suffer such judgment, what would happen to the nations surrounding Judah that did not know God? Ezekiel pronounced His judgment on them, working in a clockwise direction.

Ammon

The Ammonites, who lived on the east side of the Jordan River, descended from Lot's incest with his younger daughter (Gen. 19:30–38).

3. Skim Judges 10; 11; 1 Samuel 11; 2 Samuel 10–12. What kind of relationship did the Ammonites and Israel have during earlier times?

4. Read Ezekiel 25:3, 6. What was Ammon's attitude toward Judah when the Babylonians attacked God's people?

5. Read Ezekiel 25:5, 7. What would happen to Ammon?

6. What did God give for destroying Ammon?

In an earlier prophecy, Ezekiel had drawn a map of the ancient Near East (21:18–27). On that map was a crossroads where the king of Babylon used divination to decide whether he would first attack Ammon or Judah. He attacked Judah first.

Instead of helping God's people, the Ammonites rejoiced in their downfall (25:3, 6). In judgment, God would give Ammon to the "men of the east" (Babylon) for their possession (v. 4).

Moab

The Moabites were also Lot's children by incest (Genesis 19:30–38). They dwelled east of the Jordan but to the south of the Ammonites. During the time of the judges, Moab oppressed Israel (Judges 3). Their sin was contempt.

When the Moabites saw the destruction of Israel and said, "The house of Judah is like unto all the heathen" (Ezekiel 25:8), they denied the fulfillment of God's covenant with Abraham.

In judgment, God would open Moab to attack. Verse 9 probably refers to the plateau that made Moab almost impenetrable. Judgment from Babylon would begin at the place where the Moabites were most certain of their security.

7. Read Ezekiel 25:11. What would be the result of God's judgment on Moab?

Along with the Ammonites, the Moabites would become the possession of Babylon.

Edom

Edom was populated with the descendants of Esau. The conflict between Jacob and Esau carried through to their children on a national level. We do not know the nature of the revenge of which Ezekiel accused them in 25:12.

The writer of Psalm 137 called for God's judgment upon Edom for its vengeful spirit at the time of Jerusalem's destruction (v. 7). This may have been the last straw for Edom. God's judgment would leave Edom desolate (Ezekiel 25:13). Esau should have known and trusted the God of his father Isaac, but he chose not to. He should have respected the choice that God made to fulfill the Abrahamic Covenant through Jacob, but jealousy won out over obedience. Edom would know God's vengeance.

8. How do believers express jealousy of their brothers and sisters in Christ?

9. Are you guilty of this sin?

Philistia

The name "Philistines" is familiar to students of the Old Testament. The judges raised up armies to defeat the Philistines with varying success. These consistent enemies of the Hebrews were finally subdued by King David (2 Sam. 8). They lived on the coastal plains of the Mediterranean Sea.

10. Read Ezekiel 25:15–17. What offense had the Philistines committed against Judah?

"Old hatred" (25:15), or a long-standing feud between the Philistines and God's people, lay at the root of Philistia's judgment. The Philistines wanted to destroy the people whom God would establish as a nation. In response, God would judge them, using "great vengeance upon them with furious rebukes" (v. 17).

Tyre

Tyre received the longest prophecy of judgment. The repetition of "the word of the LORD came unto me" (26:1; 27:1; 28:1, 11) divides the judgment into four messages. Three are covered in this part of the lesson. The fourth, which deals with Satan, is covered at the end of the lesson.

Tyre was a trading city. Branching out from the seacoast, the ships of Tyre ranged through the Mediterranean and beyond. The list of those who traded with Tyre (27:12–25) and the goods they traded shows the economic power the city wielded. During the days of Solomon, King Hiram had allied with the Israelite monarchy, and both countries benefited economically (1 Kings 5:7–11).

11. Read Ezekiel 26:2. Instead of viewing the destruction of Judah with spiteful glee, Tyre saw it as an opportunity. What was that opportunity?

12. Read Ezekiel 26:7–9, 21. What inherent warning is there in Tyre's motives and subsequent judgment?

The second message against Tyre (27:1–36) is in the form of a funeral lament. In spite of Tyre's great economic power, she would be judged and destroyed. Prosperity is no refuge against the judgment of God. The picture of her ruin was a beautiful ship that founders in the sea (vv. 4ff). The "east wind" (v. 26), or Babylon, caused the ship's destruction. The ruin of such a great economic power would bring terror to the nations that benefited from Tyre (vv. 33–35).

13. Why isn't economic prosperity a refuge against God's judgment?

The third message (28:1–10) focused on the "prince of Tyrus" (v. 2). His sin was pride. As ruler of a mighty trading city, he mistakenly thought he ruled the oceans. He thought that he was a god because he had great power and wisdom (vv. 2–5). This arrogance would cost him his throne and his life (vv. 7, 8). The true God promised to bring foreign powers that would strip him of his kingdom and his life.

14. How should believers treat a powerful but arrogant public leader?

Sidon

Sidon, to the north of Tyre, had been a pain in Israel's side (28:24). However, the prophet offered no specific instances of Sidon harassing God's people. The judgment of Sidon would cause the Sidonians to know the Lord (v. 22) and thus result in glory to God. His judgment would vindicate His holiness.

The section of indictments against the nations closes with a promise of restoration for God's people. The nations that surrounded Judah would be cursed because they had cursed God's people rather than blessed them.

God's promise to regather the people of Israel from among the nations where He had scattered them is also based on the Abrahamic Covenant (Genesis 12:1–3). "They shall dwell with confidence" (Ezekiel 28:26) because God keeps His Word.

Nations are made of people. National policies are shaped by individuals. Nations today can manifest the same attitudes of the nations that surrounded Israel. The judgment of the "goat" nations at the end of the Tribulation (Matthew 25:31–46) will occur for reasons similar to God's judgment of Judah's contemporaries.

The Sponsor of National Sin

In the fourth message against Tyre, Ezekiel made a "lamentation upon the king of Tyrus" (28:12). The Hebrew word for "king" in verse 12 is different from the one used for "prince" in verse 2. The description of this "king of Tyrus" goes beyond the characteristics of any human. The clearest sense of this passage identifies the king as Satan. Satan, the "king of Tyrus," guided the human prince. Though his name is not given, his actions identify him clearly.

15. Read Ezekiel 28:13, 15. How did Satan come into existence?

16. What are the ramifications?

Satan is not all-powerful, and he is certainly not omnipresent. As a created being, he must answer to his Creator. Satan was an extraordinary creation and a model for other creatures (28:12).

17. Based on what you know about God's other created beings, what can you deduce about Satan?

Satan's wisdom was as complete as his beauty (v. 12). Nine beautiful stones graced his appearance (v. 13). He sparkled with beauty. Even now, after his fall, he can appear as an "angel of light" (2 Corinthians 11:14).

The Sponsor's Role

18. Read Ezekiel 28:14. What phrases indicate that Satan had an exalted role? What does each phrase imply about him?

Satan was anointed. He was marked out for a special task for God. This task allowed him access to "the holy mountain of God" (28:14). Thus he came into the very presence of God. What an exalted role!

Satan was the "cherub that covereth" (v. 14). The creatures under the canopy (Ezekiel 1) were also cherubs. Satan's task of "covering" may refer to some type of protection or guarding. It is possible that he guarded the throne of God. Such conjecture may miss the mark, but the closeness of Satan and God is unmistakable. As he "walked up and down in the midst of the stones of fire" (28:14), he fellowshipped with God and ministered to Him.

The Sponsor's Sin

19. Read Ezekiel 28:16, 17. What ensnared Lucifer?

20. Why did he fall?

God was not responsible for Satan's sin; his sin originated in himself (v. 15). Though we have no idea how Satan's fall occurred, we do know why it occurred. He was not content with his assigned role. His eyes fell upon himself, and he became enthralled with his own beauty and wisdom (v. 17). He used his position in Heaven for his own benefit.

All creation must submit to God. As part of creation, we must realize that God has given us all that we have. This should cause us to concentrate our thoughts on Him and lead us to give Him the glory that He deserves.

Judgment on the Sponsor

21. Read Ezekiel 28:17–19. How do we know that Satan is a defeated foe?

Satan can no longer fellowship with God. His destruction is future but guaranteed. God will humiliate him publicly and remove him from affecting anyone else. We await that day, and in the meantime live in a world where Satan influences nations.

22. Read Ephesians 6:10, 11. What is the Biblical way of protecting ourselves against attacks by Satan?

We oppose the work of Satan when we guard ourselves against the attitudes of the nations that surrounded Israel. We accept by faith that "we wrestle not against flesh and blood, but against principalities, against powers, against the rulers of the darkness of this world, against spiritual wickedness in high places" (Eph. 6:12). As our part in the battle, we must choose to "be strong in the Lord, and in the power of his might. Put on the whole armour of God, that ye may be able to stand against the wiles of the devil" (Eph. 6:10, 11).

Making It Personal

23. Do you need to confess and repent of some of the same sinful attitudes that the nations around Israel had? Are you actively demonstrating the opposite of these wrong attitudes?

24. Has your view of Satan been Biblical or manmade? Which of the following set of answers best expresses your view?

> a. Satan is comical, imaginary, harmless, and beatable by me.

> b. Satan is powerful, dangerous, the opposite of God, and beatable by me.

> c. Satan powerful, dangerous, subordinate to God, and "withstandable" through God.

25. Memorize James 4:7.

A Lesson Learned Twice

God humbles the proud.

Ezekiel 29—32

"Thus will I execute judgments in Egypt: and they shall know that I am the LORD" (Ezekiel 30:19).

Sheep's heart, liver, and lungs—they may not sound delicious to us, but Scots enjoy them in haggis. Raw seafood may not appeal to many, but others enjoy it just fine in their sushi. Deer liver, heart, and offal may not tempt our taste buds, but Medieval Britons enjoyed it in their umble pie.

As unappetizing as these dishes may sound, there's one entrée that is even less appealing, and that's the figurative one called humble pie. To eat humble pie is to be forced to admit a fault or to be humiliated. Not a dish any of us enjoys! Yet when we sin and refuse to humble ourselves, we can count on having to eat humble pie. It's a lesson we can learn from the proud nation of Egypt, as recorded in Ezekiel 29—32.

Getting Started

1. Is all pride evil?

2. What would you say is an example of bad pride?

Searching the Scriptures

During Israel's exodus from Egypt, that nation received an opportunity to submit to God. But the people were too proud to submit, and they paid a high price. Almost a thousand years later, in Ezekiel's day, Egypt again faced judgment for pride, and God revealed a three-step plan to deal with that nation.

Pride and Its Perspective

When the Bible speaks against pride, it refers to an exalted opinion of oneself. Delighting in someone else's achievements is not necessarily wrong, but developing an inaccurate view of oneself is. The only way to develop an accurate view of self is through the Scripture, where our Creator gives us an accurate picture of ourselves. If we will esteem Him highly and regard ourselves as His creatures, totally dependent on Him for all righteousness, we will begin to develop an accurate view of ourselves.

We learn from Isaiah 14:12–14 and Ezekiel 28:11–17 that Satan is the source of pride. It did not exist until he began to look upon himself improperly. He became enthralled with his own beauty and lusted after position. He forgot that his splendor was a gift from God, Who had created him.

Pride left him dissatisfied with the ministry that he had. He was no longer willing to serve God. He wanted the universe to serve him. This is the height of foolishness. The judgment against Satan was swift as he was cast out of Heaven.

No one likes to sin alone, it seems. Satan, the first sinner, immediately sought others who could be enlisted to join him in rebellion. His targets, Adam and Eve, were as perfect as he had been.

3. Read Genesis 3:1–7. What words did Satan use to appeal to Eve's pride?

4. Tell what enthralled her, what she forgot, what didn't satisfy her, what she no longer was willing to do, and what she wanted.

Satan designed his words to create a temptation to pride within Adam and Eve. He led them to believe they had the right to evaluate God's motives and commands. Passing judgment on God's Word is the ultimate example of thinking more highly of oneself than what is appropriate.

Once Adam and Eve adopted pride's perspective on reality, their sin was inevitable. They fell under the spell of self and into sin. We, their children, have walked down the same path. We must not be simplistic and say that pride is the only sin, but it does underlie many of the wrongs we commit.

5. What are some ways that people show pride?

The Dragon and the Nile

Egypt was the seventh nation against whom Ezekiel prophesied. Chapters 29—32 are composed of seven oracles, or prophetic messages, against Egypt and her ruler, Pharaoh.

Ezekiel 29:3 likens Pharaoh to a dragon (monster). The word is used to describe a wide range of reptiles, from snakes to sea monsters (Genesis 1:21). In Ezekiel, it may refer to the crocodile. The Egyptians caught crocodiles by hooking their jaws (29:4) and pulling them to land, where they were killed.

6. What enthralled the pharaoh of Egypt? (Ezekiel 29:3)

7. What did he forget?

In judgment, the true Creator promised to take Pharaoh away from the Nile to death in the desert (v. 5). He would be left for the vultures, not having burial in the traditional tombs of the Pharaohs. The Egyptian people would face judgment with him. The "fish of thy rivers" in verse 5 refers to them.

8. Read Ezekiel 29:6–8. What were God's purposes in judging Egypt?

When Judah decided to rebel against Babylon, Egypt agreed to ally with Judah and protect her. But Egypt failed to deliver on her diplomatic promises.

9. According to Ezekiel 29:9–14, how long would Egypt be in captivity?

10. What kind of nation would she be after her people returned to the land?

Judgment would fall for Pharaoh's claim to be the originator and owner of the Nile (v. 9). God promised judgment for the whole land. "Syene" is on the South Nile, and Ethiopia was the southern border of Egypt (v. 10). Thus the whole land to the border farthest from Judah would face God's wrath.

11. What does Ezekiel 29:15 indicate Egypt wanted that God would not allow her to have again?

The Lord would cause "the horn of the house of Israel to bud forth" (v. 21) because of Egypt's destruction. A horn usually symbolizes strength or power. As Israel suffered in captivity, the destruction of Egypt would give her strength. She would realize that God's word always comes to pass.

After Egypt's restoration, Egyptians would inhabit only the northern portion of their land. Stripped of power and influence, the country would never wield the world power that she had had for centuries (v. 15). God's grace even in judgment remained the same. He wanted the Egyptians to know Him (v. 16).

Tyre Too

Ezekiel 19 records God's judgment on Tyre (vv. 17–21) and indirectly on Egypt. Babylon's siege of Tyre was long and difficult (v. 18), for Tyre was aided by Egypt, both to resist the attack and to relocate Tyre's wealth. When Babylon finally took Tyre, the cost of the siege was so great that the plunder from the city did not offset it. But the Lord, Who controls the destinies of nations, later gave the riches of Egypt to Nebuchadnezzar in return for his earlier defeat/judgment of Tyre.

Egypt's Disgrace

Ezekiel 30 and 31 reveal how God would humble proud Egypt and her pharaoh.

12. What are ways God humbles the proud?

13. Describe a time when God used one of these ways to humble you.

Egypt's allies (v. 6) would fall, and then Nebuchadnezzar would burn Egypt (vv. 10, 14). The Egyptian idols would pass from existence (v. 13). The plagues of Moses' day had shown that Egyptian idols had no power against the true God. Yet for over a thousand years after Moses, Egypt had continued to trust in her worthless gods.

City by city, Ezekiel described the complete destruction of the Egyptian empire (vv. 13–18). Ezekiel ended the message of judgment as he had started it with an image of clouds (vv. 3, 18). The day of God's judgment on Egypt was a cloudy, gloomy day. However, as always, God's judgment manifests His grace. Through judgment, the Egyptians would come to understand that the Lord is God (v. 19).

14. What nations today are particularly worrisome to our country?

15. How should believers think and respond?

Ezekiel also predicted that the Egyptians would be scattered and dispersed, much as seed is cast randomly into the field. The repetition in verses 23 and 26 highlights the finality of the judgment. Their nation destroyed and their gods proven useless, the Egyptians would once again know that the Lord is truly God.

16. Why doesn't contemporary Egypt know that God is the Lord?

17. What's the inherent warning for us as Christians?

18. What's the inherent warning for our nation?

19. What evidences from antiquity demonstrate that Egypt was once a mighty power?

In 31:1–9, Ezekiel presented a beautiful poem about the greatness of Egypt. He compared Egypt to Assyria, implying Egypt's superiority. Assyria was one of the old rivals to Egypt for power, but the Assyrian Empire had been destroyed by Babylon. Egypt, too, would be destroyed; God would humble her through destruction.

God is able to humble proud nations that ignore Him. Several of the nations that Ezekiel prophesied against were major economic powers. Assyria, Babylon, and Egypt were also political powers. When God decided that their arrogance had gone far enough, He brought them down. Their destruction was as sudden as it was devastating.

A Lament

Ezekiel had already delivered laments for Judah (Ezekiel 19) and Tyre (Ezekiel 27). He then delivered one for Egypt (32:1–10).

20. What is a lament or a "lamentation"?

Usually, a lament would be sung at a funeral. Though Egypt was not yet judged, her future was sealed. Ezekiel likened Pharaoh's attempts to fight the growing influence of Babylon as a troubling of the waters by the crocodile (v. 2). Though the great reptile is fearsome and can churn the waters mightily, Egypt would not prevail. In accord with God's prophecy, the crocodile was drawn from the Nile and slaughtered.

Ezekiel 32:11–16 gives the interpretation of the prophecy of 32:1–10. The figurative expressions give way to harsh reality. Babylon would judge Egypt. The Nile would quiet in the wake of the deportation and slaughter. Pharaoh would be killed and his government ended. "Then shall they know that I am the LORD" (v. 15). The God Who keeps His word to His people kept His word to Pharaoh too.

Ezekiel's final prophecy against Egypt (vv. 17–32) was also his final prophecy against the nations. He predicted the arrival of Egypt in "the pit," which is a figurative expression for the grave, or death. Egypt would join all the formerly great powers of the world. Not one nation can exalt itself against the Lord. All powers will submit to Him in one way or another. Egypt and the nations submitted to His mighty hand of judgment. They had no choice.

How much better it would have been to respond to the grace of God! He is willing to forgive the sins of the humble. Pharaoh never learned the lesson that God sent prophets to teach him. James summarized the principle well: "But he giveth more grace. Wherefore he saith, God resisteth the proud, but giveth grace unto the humble" (James 4:6).

Making It Personal

21. Are you enthralled with someone/something other than God? Have you forgotten who you truly are? Have you become dissatisfied with something? What? Is there something you are no longer willing to do? What? Is there something you want more than you want God and Christlikeness? In short, is your pride heading you for judgment?

22. What are three Bible verses that could help you humble yourself before God and submit to Him? Choose one to memorize and meditate upon.

23. Memorize Ezekiel 30:19.

Turn toward Life!

*We please God when we deliberately choose
obedience over hypocrisy and pride.*

Ezekiel 33

**"Say unto them, As I live, saith the Lord GOD,
I have no pleasure in the death of the wicked;
but that the wicked turn from his way and live:
turn ye, turn ye from your evil ways" (Ezekiel
33:11a).**

A young lady was running late for church, so she hurried to get herself and her family out the door. They hurried just enough to make it on time and avoid the embarrassment of being late. However, the embarrassment of being late didn't seem so bad to the mom after she walked into the church. That was because she was wearing one black shoe and one blue shoe. In her hurrying she chose two mismatched shoes. To make matters worse, the shoes were completely different styles. She made a bad choice that she couldn't change.

Sometimes our choices in life aren't so permanent. Turning from sin to God is a choice that we can make immediately.

Getting Started

1. What decisions have you made that required you to turn to one thing/person and away from others?

2. Why aren't such choices always permanent?

Ezekiel had warned that judgment was coming, but he had another message as well: turn from sin to God!

Searching the Scriptures

The exiles in Babylon pretended to be interested in and respectful of Ezekiel's messages from God, but their reverence was hypocritical. And their hypocrisy kept them from truly turning to God—in spite of three motivations for living righteously.

The Watchman's Warning (33:1–9)

3. What do you recall about a watchman's responsibility from lesson 2 on Ezekiel 3:16–21?

4. What did his responsibilities include?

5. What did they not include?

Ezekiel 33:1–7 sounds like a repetition of Ezekiel's commissioning, when he was appointed a watchman for Judah (3:16–21). This section repeats some of those responsibilities, but as the prelude to a more positive ministry. The watchman would warn people of their sin and call them to righteousness. In this way, Ezekiel 33 teaches some important truths about the role of a prophet.

Remember that this watchman's role does not pertain to a warning about eternal life or eternal death. Instead, the prophet warned the nation to obey God or to face the physical death that He promised for disobedience. That death would come at the hand of an invading nation.

6. Read Romans 15:14; Colossians 3:16; 1 Thessalonians 5:11; Hebrews 3:13. What do the words "admonish," "edify," and "exhort" mean?

7. How does being a watchman apply to believers today?

Just as Ezekiel accepted his role in Israel, we must accept our role of exhortation in each others' lives. We have a responsibility to assist each other in growth.

8. Why does a "watchman" today have to warn instead of simply pray?

Many believers shrink from the thought of giving another believer a direct warning. They would willingly pray for the erring brother, hoping that prayer alone would change his actions. Prayer is fundamental, but exhortation and rebuke are also essential.

When we see other believers transgress the clear teachings of God's Word, we must help them understand their error. A careful study of the Word, along with loving application of it, may help a brother or sister find the right path again. We are to minister to others in the Body of Christ to help them grow.

9. Read Ephesians 4:11–16. Is warning individual believers primarily the responsibility of pastors or of all believers?

10. Why might you shrink from being a watchman?

A key part of a pastor's responsibility is training the saints to do the work of the ministry. If church members are unwilling to accept their responsibility to minister, their church will remain immature.

The Lord gave Ezekiel a responsibility to his fellow Jews, but God also limited Ezekiel's responsibility. God did not require him to produce obedience in someone else's life. He was to speak and warn. If some chose to ignore his warning, Ezekiel was not responsible for that. We take on more responsibility than God intended us to have if we attempt to control the listener's response.

11. Why should believers today listen to those who warn them?

The watchman's warning is a powerful motive for right living.

The Pleasure of God

12. Read Ezekiel 33:10, 11. What does God take pleasure in?

At this point the Lord gave Ezekiel hope. Repeatedly Ezekiel had warned the sinful people of the consequence of their choices. He had revealed the shattering judgment to come. Judah faced God's terrible judgment, but some of the people were considering the implications of the prophet's words. The watchman's warning had moved their hearts to fear. They did not want to face God's chastisement for their actions. Their only hope was to rid themselves of their sins.

Three times in verse 11 God commanded the Jews to "turn." The physical motion of turning pictures the mental choice necessary for repentance. When people "turn" their minds away from sin, they decide that sin is wrong and that they want to do right.

It was not necessary for the Jews to die—they could please the Lord! God's word showed them the evils they had practiced. They knew with certainty both the reason for judgment and the path of restoration and righteousness. They could please the Lord by repentance.

13. How does/should a believer's motivation to live righteously differ from an unbeliever's motivation?

14. Why is it important to know that God takes pleasure in repentance?

The Judgment of Works

Through Ezekiel, the Lord reaffirmed His previous teachings. God requires righteousness. If a righteous person turns his back on righteousness and begins to sin, he will be judged. His past obedience cannot offset the change in his heart (33:12, 13). On the other hand, those who live unrighteously but repent and begin to live according to God's Word will be rewarded (33:14–16).

The words "life" and "death" in Ezekiel 33 refer to physical life and death. The covenant between God and Israel was specific (Deuteronomy 30:19, 20).

The people of Judah should have known the requirements of blessing, which were written in the law.

15. Why is God's reward of good works so motivating for right living?

We have seen that Ezekiel offered three motivations to "turn and live": first, the warning from the watchman to repent; second, the desire to please God; and third, the judgment of works. But as God's people turn from sin to God, they do not have an easy time.

16. Why isn't repenting (turning from sin to God) easy?

One day a messenger arrived bearing news of Jerusalem's downfall (Ezekiel 33:21, 22). As the Lord had promised, this news ended the period when Ezekiel was unable to speak. The city's downfall was the proof of God's judgment. Yet God's Chosen People still struggled with repentance.

The Barrier of Pride

Ezekiel's countrymen made a foolish analogy (33:23, 24). Since Abraham (one man) had possessed the land, they thought they, too, would possess the land. The sheer weight of their numbers ought to work in their favor, they thought. But they forgot that Abraham possessed the land by his faith. Their disobedience demonstrated their lack of faith. They had Abraham as their biological father, but that genetic tie would not qualify them for possession of the land. The Children of Israel had to come to God on His standards, not on their own rationalization. Their lives were marked by disobedience to specific commandments of God.

17. Read Ezekiel 33:25, 26. What direct violations of God's commands were the Jews guilty of?

These are not violations of obscure portions of God's law; they violate some of God's core concerns for righteous living.

18. What question did God ask twice in Ezekiel 33:25, 26?

19. Why did God ask the question twice?

Judah's pride in religious tradition (Abraham) would soon be crushed by the reality of God's judgment. It was this pride that was keeping the Jews from true repentance (vv. 27, 28).

20. How do we feel when we keep certain religious rules that we have set up through traditions?

21. In addition to their religious tradition, what were the Jews taking pride in (Ezekiel 33:26a)?

God had promised in Deuteronomy 28:7 to meet all their defense needs. All they had to do was live a righteous life. Instead, they chose self-reliance.

Though the Jews were Abraham's children and they were numerous, they lacked the qualifications to possess the land. God hates pride. It replaces the true standard (God) with a false one (self).

The Barrier of Hypocrisy

Far from Jerusalem, the exiles could no longer conduct their religious life as they had at home. As a substitute for their accustomed religious patterns, they regularly came to hear Ezekiel. They listened to him, commented on his word, but made no change in their lives.

Their show of religion was hypocritical. They regularly sat before Ezekiel. They even invited others to come and hear him (Ezekiel 33:30, 31). Yet they did not listen. They enjoyed the religious experience, ignoring the truth that Ezekiel spoke.

Their reverence was hypocritical. They listened to Ezekiel and they loved to hear his words. They praised his manner of speaking and his speaking voice (33:32). The casual watcher might think that wonderful things were resulting from Ezekiel's ministry, considering the regular attendance and the devotion of the people.

Years later, James delivered a similar warning to the church. "But be ye doers of the word, and not hearers only, deceiving your own selves. . . . But whoso looketh into the perfect law of liberty, and continueth therein, he being not a forgetful hearer, but a doer of the work, this man shall be blessed in his deed" (James 1:22, 25). We, like the children of Israel, can manifest the hypocrisy that destroys true religion.

God's judgment was certain. After it came, the truth of Ezekiel's words, and therefore the vindication of his ministry, would be a public fact. When God offers the opportunity to repent, along with such motivation as Ezekiel 33 contains, who could desire to remain far from Him?

Making It Personal

22. Turning to God is an action based on a choice, and it isn't done once for all. Evaluate your desire to turn to God. Make a note of the following statements that apply to you.

_____ I have let religious pride keep me from wholly trusting God.

_____ I have let self-reliance keep me from wholly yielding to God.

_____ I have been hypocritical, listening but not changing.

_____ I am open to admonition, rebuke, etc. from fellow believers (watchmen).

_____ I desire to please God.

_____ I want works that will withstand the Judgment Seat of Christ.

23. If you are serious about repenting, write a prayer of commitment.

24. Have you been shirking your responsibility to admonish, edify, and exhort your brother and sisters in Christ? What can you do to strengthen yourself in this duty?

25. Memorize Ezekiel 33:11.

Reassurance and Restoration

God restores the repentant.

Ezekiel 34—37

"And shall put my spirit in you, and ye shall live, and I shall place you in your own land: then shall ye know that I the LORD have spoken it, and performed it, saith the LORD" (Ezekiel 37:14).

The longest word found in a major dictionary is "pneumonoultramicroscopicsilicovolcanoconiosis." It is a technical term that represents a lung disease associated with volcanic ash. To say the word without pausing takes a lot of practice.

The words "I was wrong" are easy to read but much harder to say than the long word above. Admitting that we are in need of forgiveness is not in our nature. Shifting blame or running from our wrongs is easier to do.

Getting Started

1. How do you feel when you know you must apologize?

2. Describe a creative, resourceful method of apologizing.

3. What response(s) from the other person lets you know that the apology has been accepted?

Today's study will examine the way God will restore Israel. We'll learn three truths about Him. In His restoration of Israel, we also see the pattern He uses to restore us individually.

Searching the Scriptures

The Lord Is Our Shepherd

4. What are at least four responsibilities of a shepherd?

5. How are spiritual leaders like shepherds?

Ezekiel 34 and 35 begin with a scathing indictment of Israel's leadership (34:1–10). These "shepherds" took care of themselves only. Citing examples of their mistreatment of "the flock," the Lord accused the leaders of using the privileges of leadership to enrich themselves.

6. Read Ezekiel 34:1–6. Why did God consider the Jewish leaders to be bad shepherds?

The shepherds fed themselves, not the flock, and they ignored the needs of God's people. They didn't help the weak or treat the sick. Though the sheep were scattered, the shepherds did not seek them to bring them back to safety. The nation was scattered because the shepherds had failed in their task (vv. 2–6).

God promised judgment upon these leaders. Once He removed the leaders from their role, they themselves would need a competent, caring shepherd. He would take this responsibility (vv. 8–10).

Shepherds Lead, Satisfy, Protect

7. Read Ezekiel 34:11–16. What characterized the Good Shepherd?

The Lord would rescue the scattered sheep and lead them back to their land. No matter how far away or desolate, not one of His children would be forgotten. He would lead them to the Promised Land (v. 14). Even though they thoroughly deserved their judgment, He did not decide to scrap His covenant with them. He never would, for it is based on His character and promise. He would deny Himself if He denied His Word.

Back in their land, God Himself would feed, safeguard, and heal His people. He would satisfy their needs. However, He would just as personally judge those who had taken advantage of the sheep, who were fat and strong at the others' expense (vv. 15, 16).

Ezekiel 34:17–22 refers to two judgments. God will judge between the sheep, and then between the sheep and the goats. Judging those who have harmed Israel is one way of protecting the nation. Matthew 25:31–34 and 41 reveals that the sheep will inherit the Kingdom (v. 34), and the goats will be cursed, sent away from God "into everlasting fire."

This judgment will take place at the end of the Tribulation. The Lord will deliver Israel from all predators (Ezekiel 34:22), whether they are members of the Hebrew nation (sheep) or foreign nations (goats). He will judge the nations based on their treatment of His people.

When Israel submits to the Lord as her God, the problems of justice will fall into place. Her first act of submission will be to yield to God's rule. After that, she will trust Him to care for her completely.

The Lord will also protect His people by providing security. He will make peace between Israel and the wild animals. According to verse 28, this is not merely a picture of Israel's national neighbors. God will actually keep the nation safe from the wild animals of the land. He will also restore covenant conditions in agriculture. The land will return to productivity and beauty. Famine will be a thing of the past (v. 26).

God will also allow the people to live in peace with their neighbors. God will no longer use these nations to chastise His people. Once again, they will enjoy the respect of the nations. Jesus is the Good Shepherd. As the messianic King of the nation, He will supply the leadership that Israel lacked and will satisfy her completely.

8. What verses in the New Testament reveal Jesus Christ as the believer's Shepherd? (See John 10.)

9. Describe ways in which He has shepherded you.

The Lord Is Our Avenger

10. Read Ezekiel 36:1–15. What had become of the land of Israel?

11. How will God reverse this?

Other nations gossiped about the destruction of the once-powerful Israel (36:3). They plundered and ridiculed the land (v. 4). They should have learned from the judgment of Israel. If they had repented of their sins and humbled themselves before God, He would have turned judgment away from them.

Having promised to judge the nations who had judged Israel, the Lord promised to restore the Land of Promise. The Jewish people will return. Most importantly, God will restore the nation's testimony (vv. 13–15).

God will also avenge His people by changing their hearts. Other countries might understand Israel's return to national prominence. After all, other nations have come back from devastation. But God's regenerating work in the hearts of His people will show that Israel's restoration is more than shrewd politics.

The sins of Israel repulsed the Lord, and He kept His Word to judge her for her sins. Yet the nations where the exiles lived misunderstood the Lord's judgment. They thought that He was weak when His people were driven from His land to theirs. God's name, or reputation, suffered at the captivity of His people. But He will restore both His people and His reputation.

12. Read Ezekiel 36:24–28. What steps will the Lord take to restore His people and His reputation?

These steps God will take to restore His people are unique to Israel. That is obvious by the simple fact that we as church-age believers do not have a physical land to which God will restore us. Our hope is Heaven, not a restored Promised Land.

13. While the church, the Body of Christ (i.e., all believers in this age), won't receive this kind of restoration, is God still the avenger of believers? (See Romans 12:19; 2 Thessalonians 1:7–9; and Hebrews 10:30.)

The Lord Is Our Life

In addition to being Israel's shepherd and avenger, God is Israel's life. He vividly portrayed this truth in one of the most famous visions in the Bible. It is recorded in Ezekiel 37.

The Spirit of God brought Ezekiel to a valley where he was surrounded by dried bones. He described the situation with two superlatives: the bones were very dry and very many in number (37:2).

The Lord posed a question: "Can these bones live?" Ezekiel had learned that God is not limited, and he hedged in giving his answer (v. 3). From the human perspective, nothing could bring the bones back to life.

But, as directed, Ezekiel preached a message of promise and hope to the bones. In his vision, Ezekiel heard a noise first. The bones, rattling, moved into position to form skeletons. Next, Ezekiel watched as complete bodies were formed from the bones out to the skin. The perfectly formed bodies lacked only life, and God then gave them breath.

14. What did the dry bones' being made living men represent in regards to Israel?

Just as God gave life to the bones in Ezekiel's vision, God gives life to those who believe on Him for salvation.

15. Read Ephesians 2:1–10. What one word describes everyone spiritually, unless that person believes on Jesus Christ?

16. What happens spiritually to those who receive Jesus Christ?

17. How should believers respond to the fact that the Lord is our life?

God made us alive (v. 5) even when we were dead in our transgressions. If not for His rich and free grace, we would still be spiritually dead. He began His mighty work in our lives at our point of need. We lacked life; He supplied it. In the face of such a wonderful intrusion into our lives, we should give ourselves wholly to serve Him.

18. Read Ezekiel 37:11–14. How much of Israel would God bring to spiritual life?

19. How will the Jews then differ from those in Ezekiel's day?

God promised to bring spiritual life to His people, but He also promised to restore their national life. In spite of the sorry conditions of the people, God promised a reunited political entity. The regathering of the Israelites would make such a kingdom possible. Unlike the days of the divided kingdom, one ruler would reign. Their spiritual life would be strong. The cleansed people would no longer worship idols. They would cling to God alone.

Twice in Ezekiel 37:12–14, the Lord promised a resurrection for the nation. The people will come to life, return to the land, and be united as one nation. The Davidic king, the Messiah, will rule, and God's presence will return to the temple. God's promises for His people focused on the land that He had promised to Abraham for an eternal possession. The people's idolatry had taken them far from the land in judgment.

One day the people of Israel will be bound to God forever by a covenant of peace. Once again, they will enjoy the presence of God's sanctuary. As a holy nation, they will be a living testimony to the presence and work of God.

Ezekiel 37 is exactly what a premillennialist would expect. There will be a literal fulfillment of the promises that God made to Israel.

Some may doubt this. How could the nation come to faith and be returned to her ancestral home? How could Israel return to prominence? The answer is in the miraculous power of God's Word. Israel will respond to God's Messiah during the tribulation period. As she turns to Him, He will open a fountain of cleansing for her (Zechariah 13:1). The promises of God will be fulfilled literally. This great hope for Israel's future is also a great hope for our future. We will rule and reign with Christ in the Kingdom (2 Timothy 2:11, 12).

Making It Personal

20. If you have never believed in Jesus Christ as your Savior from the penalty of sin, you are still spiritually dead. Will you receive Him as your personal Savior right now?

21. If you're a leader anywhere, in a sense you are a shepherd and those who follow you are your flock. Are you more like the bad shepherds of Ezekiel's day or like the Good Shepherd?

22. What difficulties are you facing?

23. How can knowing that God is your shepherd, your avenger, and the giver of life comfort you and help you in a practical way?

24. Memorize Ezekiel 37:14.

The Biggest Mistake the Gog Could Make

God demonstrates His holiness when He fulfills His word.

Ezekiel 38; 39

"So will I make my holy name known in the midst of my people Israel; and I will not let them pollute my holy name any more: and the heathen shall know that I am the LORD, the Holy One in Israel" (Ezekiel 39:7).

Preliminary bombing began on March 19, 2003, but was followed two days later with a "shock and awe" assault. The United States and her allies launched more than 1,600 air raids, about a third of which were from cruise missiles. Coalition ground forces seized Baghdad on April 5.

Getting Started

1. What does this paragraph describe?

2. How do you know?

3. If you had read this article in 1776 or even in 1956, what details would have made no sense to you?

Ezekiel 38 and 39 contain some confusing material—but only because we do not have all the data yet. A time is coming when these chapters will read like a newspaper. Though we lack some specifics, we can gain by studying these chapters.

Searching the Scriptures

Ezekiel 38 and 39 are part of the end-time calendar. After the Lord Jesus returns to earth and establishes the millennial Kingdom for Israel, He will reign for one thousand years. During that time, conditions similar to the Garden of Eden will prevail on earth. A perfect King will govern perfectly. Satan, bound in the pit, will not torment men or nations. What a wonderful time!

At the end of the Millennium, Satan will be released from his prison. In spite of the wonders of the preceding years, he will be able to incite a rebellion against the King, the Lord Jesus. The nations in the four corners of the earth, Gog, and Magog, will attack Israel. Living in millennial peace, Israel will be defenseless—except for God. Because He is holy, He will defend His people.

Experts on the doctrine of last things, or eschatology, have puzzled for years over the identity of Gog and Magog. Ezekiel reveals little about their identity but reveals much about their character. Chapters 38 and 39 show the marked contrast between the unbelieving nations and our holy God. Though we may wonder about the identity of God's opponents, we find repeated truth about our God: He is holy.

Holiness Is Separateness

4. What thoughts come to your mind when you think about the holiness of God?

The term "holiness" contains the idea of "distinction," "apartness" or "separateness." God is holy. He is entirely and uniquely pure in His nature. He is totally good. Evil does not pertain to him. His holiness is a part of his nature.

5. Can a thing be holy? Explain.

For everything and everyone but God, holiness is derived. "Things" are not holy by nature. They are holy because of their use. For example, the vessels of the tabernacle and temple were holy. They were reserved for worship use alone.

6. Read Numbers 16:36–38. What made the censers used by Korah, Dathan, and Abiram holy when the men themselves were unholy?

7. Are people holy by nature? Explain.

Holiness is not a part of our being, but is a gift from God. The Lord commanded both Israel and the church to be holy (Leviticus 19:2; 1 Peter 1:16). This command sounds like a shortcut to frustration unless we understand holiness correctly. Just as God is set apart to His purposes, we are to be set apart to His purposes. We become unique by our desire to accomplish His design in His way. Holiness naturally leads to a desire for righteousness, which in turn produces purity. A holy person is one who has determined to become sacred, set apart for use by God.

Holiness Generates a Testimony

The word "sanctified" means "shown to be holy." It is used in the same way in Ezekiel 38:23.

8. Read Ezekiel 38:16, 23; 39:27. What does holiness generate among "the heathen" and "many nations"?

9. Read Romans 12:1; Ephesians 1:4; 1 Peter 1:15, 16; 2:9. What does God expect from believers?

10. When do unbelievers know that you as a believer are holy?

It may seem impossible, but God can show His holiness through humans. When God regathers the Jews from the corners of the earth, regenerates them, and re-creates them as a nation, they will demonstrate His holiness by their lives.

We Church-age saints also display His holiness when our lives are marked by His work in us.

Holiness Reveals Incomparability

11. What is the significance of God's making the nations "know that [He is] the LORD"? (See Ezekiel 38:16 and 23 and 39:27.)

Gog's great error will lie ultimately in ignoring the holiness of God. Because God is holy, He will do what He promises; He will do it exactly the way He promised He would. When God keeps His Word, He proves His holiness. Therefore, God's restoration of Israel will be a manifestation of His holiness. Similarly, He shows His holiness when He judges the nations.

12. Read Ezekiel 38:19–23. What phenomena of nature will happen against Gog?

The attack of Gog upon Israel will arouse God's anger. This final assault on His people will prompt a display of God's incomparability and holiness. The terrors of God's judgment (v. 22) will reveal that He is the true Master of the world. The nation of Israel and the nations of the earth can come to no other conclusion. When God shows His holiness, they will recognize Him for Who He is (v. 23).

Holiness Brings about Fellowship

God promised to make His holy name known among His people (39:7). The word "name" refers to His character and reputation. When God's name is polluted or taken in vain and profaned, He is demeaned. Those who show Him disrespect cannot fellowship with Him. It's not possible to fellowship with one you do not respect.

13. In general, do people share a close relationship with those whose names they take in vain? Explain.

14. What does taking God's name in vain reflect about the person who does it?

God will accomplish the restoration of Israel (vv. 25, 26). He will bring her back from captivity. This is grace in action, for Israel's sins against God made her captivity just and appropriate. This restoration is not merely an obligation that God will fulfill as one might complete a contractual obligation. It is an act of His compassion. He loves and cares for His people, in spite of their sin.

After God purifies Israel, the nation will enjoy His fellowship again (vv. 28, 29). His holy character will be a part of Israel's national life; and His holy presence, the source of the nation's joy.

15. How is God's holy character a source of joy for you?

16. How is God's holy character a motivation for you?

17. Name some practical ways we believers can grow in our understanding of God's holiness.

Gog's Preparations

We don't know particulars about "Gog, the chief prince of Meshech and Tubal" (Ezek. 39:1). His name also appears in Revelation 20:8. Gog is from the land of Magog, which is not identified either. Meshech and Tubal were the grandsons of Noah through Japheth. As nearly as we can determine, they settled by the Black Sea.

Because Gog will attack "out of the north parts" (38:15), some have identified Gog as a Russian ruler. Magog, then, would be Russia. In addition, some note the similarity in sound between Meshech and Moscow. When they find that the Hebrew word for "prince" is *rosh,* the similarity in sound to "Russia" seals the case for them. But the fact that the attack will come from the north doesn't prove that Gog is Russia any more than it proves that Ethiopia is Russia.

Though we know little about Gog, we know much about his plan. He will organize a large, well-armed coalition of armies. According to both Ezekiel 38 and Revelation 20, it will come from all the peoples of the earth. Gog will command a vast force (38:7).

The time of the attack is indefinite (38:8), but Ezekiel places it at a time when the nation of Israel has lived at peace. This corresponds well to the account in Revelation, which makes it clear that the attack will come after the millennial rule of Christ. During His Kingdom, the Lord will return Edenic conditions to the earth. All mankind's needs will be met. Justice will be dispensed perfectly by the perfect King.

Because of the conditions of Christ's Kingdom, Israel will be unfortified. Three times Ezekiel 38 emphasizes the safety and security of Israel (vv. 8, 11, 14). Those who have a right relationship to God will live securely (Leviticus 25:18; Psalm 16:9). The presence of the Christ will meet all of their needs.

However, Gog will not be a believer. He will be unaware of the source of Israel's security. Instead, he will see a nation of fools. They will be rich but will have no obvious protection. So he will gather the armies to plunder riches that seem unprotected.

Gog will come from the far north (Ezekiel 38:15). He will advance like a storm (38:9). His army will cover the land like a cloud (v. 16). The opposition to God's King and Kingdom will be massive.

God's Vengeance

But appearances are deceptive. Israel's defense will lie not in walled cities but in the covenant she has with God. Though Gog will not know it, his rebellion against Messiah's Kingdom will bring about the complete fulfillment of God's promises to Israel.

18. When have you seen God faithfully vindicate His people before unbelievers?

Glorious in Judgment

The nations that surrounded Israel believed that their gods were greater than the one true God. After all, they had bested Israel in battle. Surely their gods, therefore, had bested Israel's God. They did not know that the Babylonian Captivity was God's chastisement of His people. Far from showing God's weakness, it demonstrated His willingness to fulfill His Word.

19. What is glory?

20. How can judging Gog and Magog showcase God's glory?

Ultimately, Gog's plans will fall under the sovereign plan of God. Though Gog will look on Israel as a nation ripe to plunder, God will use Gog's sin to glorify Himself.

The Lord will cause Gog to fall. The vultures will feast on the fallen of his army. Judgment from God will have the same effect then as it had in Egypt thousands of years ago (39:6, 7). God will turn the tables on Gog's army. The weapons that they intended to use to kill God's people will be a source of fuel for seven years (v. 9). Those who planned to loot Israel will instead become the supply of plunder for Israel.

The task of cleansing the land will take time and labor. For seven months, the people of Israel will bury the slain (v. 12). After that, a smaller group will go throughout the land looking for less obvious remains to bury.

The burial of Gog himself will specially remind Israel of God's work on their behalf. God will be glorified (v. 13) because He will have kept His promise. No living enemy will remain. Even the months of toil to remove the uncleanness of death from the land will be a daily lesson: "God has kept His Word to us!"

Glorious in Restoration

21. How will restoring Israel demonstrate God's glory?

God will display His glory as He works on Israel's behalf (39:21). First, He will restore her knowledge of Him. His presence in her midst and His judgment on her behalf will bring her to final knowledge. He is the only God, the true God, and ultimately, Israel's God. Her relationship with Him is secure.

Second, the Lord will restore His people's reputation (39:26, 27). The Israelites had lived shamefully and had reaped the results of that choice for generations. Third, God's work will bring them to holiness and purity before the nations. The past will be washed away. Because of the work of God, their reputation will be changed. In addition to erasing the shame of the past, the Lord will give Israel the opportunity to be a testimony for Him. By His work for her, He will show His holiness through her.

Making It Personal

22. How has God's holiness as seen in Ezekiel 38 and 39 influenced you to be holy?

23. How has your personal holiness affected your testimony? Your incomparability? Your fellowship with God?

24. Write a memo to yourself to remind you of a specific area of holiness in which you want to improve. Include at least one specific way that the improvement could come to pass.

25. Memorize Ezekiel 39:7.

Lesson 13

Home Again!

Worship of God is the proper response after restoration from sin.

Ezekiel 40—48

"And the name of the city from that day shall be, The Lord is there" (Ezekiel 48:35b).

Ａnd the prince and the princess lived happily ever after. The end."

Many fairly tales end with those words, but while we still live in a world of sin and pain, "happily ever after" seems like mere wishful thinking. However, just such an ending is coming. After the cleansing of the final battles of the Tribulation, the Messiah will rule. He will restore the world to conditions like those in Eden. That "happily ever after" will actually be happy forever after.

Getting Started

1. Describe an event from your own life that seemed like a "happily ever after" ending because the Lord graciously allowed life to work out much better than it had seemed it might.

2. Would you want to live "happily ever after" on this earth in your present condition? Why or why not?

In today's study, we will learn details concerning that "happily ever after" day.

Searching the Scriptures

A Place to Worship

Ezekiel devoted almost one-fifth of his book to a description of the conditions in millennial Israel. Much of the material in chapters 40—48 is minute detail, measuring the dimensions of the temple and land allotments. Why devote so much time to such precision? Perhaps Ezekiel was balancing the material on the terrible reality of God's judgment, in the earlier chapters, with material on the wonderful reality of God's restoration in chapters 40—48.

This vision of Ezekiel's took place in the twenty-fifth year of the captivity of Judah, approximately 573 BC. In the vision, Ezekiel returned to Jerusalem as he had in chapters 8—11. Beginning with 40:3, a man "whose appearance was like the appearance of brass" took Ezekiel through the temple that will be built for God's restored people. The measurements are very detailed, providing a clear floor plan.

The measuring standard was the cubit, but Ezekiel may have used the regular cubit (18 in.) or the long cubit (21 in.). Thus, we cannot give the dimensions with precision, but we do know the basic shape.

The temple he saw had an outer court and an inner court. The rooms around the outer court formed three sides of a square on the north, south, and east sides. Gates allowed access to the outer court on these same sides. Enclosed inside the outer court was the inner court. This contained the temple proper. As with the outer court, gates provided access from the north, south, and east. The temple itself was twice as long as it was wide.

The millennial temple will have a holy place (41:4). The priests who will minister to the Lord will wear holy garments. After they minister, they will change out of the holy garments. They will eat a portion of the sacrifices, so their food will be holy food (42:13, 14). Once again, God's people will appreciate the difference between sacred and secular. That which is totally devoted to God will have no common use. It will be reserved entirely for Him.

Is this all real? Yes, and the presence of line after line of specific dimensions helps us to understand its reality.

3. When have you seen or heard Christians saying that God has rejected Israel because the nation rejected Jesus Christ when He was on earth?

4. How do they explain away the covenants God made with Abraham, Isaac, and Jacob?

5. How could that view affect Christians' view of modern-day Israel?

Some Christians do teach that God rejected Israel and made the church the new Israel. The literal promises that the Lord made to Abraham, Isaac, Jacob, and Israel then become figurative, interpreted to pertain to the church.

However, every one of Ezekiel's prophecies to this point in the book had a literal fulfillment. On what basis would we suddenly change our interpretation system to make these prophecies nonliteral? The Bible does not teach that God has rejected His covenant people and replaced them with the church. We should expect King Jesus, our Savior, to rule for a millennium, just as the book of Revelation predicts. We should also expect a millennial temple. Its size and shape will match the careful measurements noted by Ezekiel.

6. Since believers are the temple of the Holy Spirit for the Church Age, what "equipment" do we have to use for worshiping the Lord?

A Presence to Worship

7. Read Ezekiel 9:3; 10:4, 18, 19. What had happened to the glory of the Lord?

8. Read Ezekiel 43:2–5. What will happen to the glory of the Lord in the Millennium?

The messenger who was conducting Ezekiel through the temple brought him to the east gate. As the prophet stood there, he saw the glory of God returning from the east, the direction it had departed. In humility, Ezekiel fell on his face in worship (43:1–3).

The glory had come at the dedication of the tabernacle in the wilderness (Exodus 40:34, 35) and at the dedication of Solomon's temple (1 Kings 8:10, 11). As the glory of the Lord filled the house in Ezekiel's vision, the Lord Himself interpreted the vision for Ezekiel. Even though this looked similar to the previous dedications, a great difference marked this event.

9. Read Ezekiel 43:7. What will be different in the Millennium and millennial temple from Israel's life on earth and her past temples?

The Lord instructed Ezekiel to explain the entire temple plan to the people. Imagine the hope that would result. As God's people languished in their captivity, the prophet received specific building plans for a magnificent temple.

10. How do you think the people responded to hearing the minute details of the millennial temple?

11. How should the plans for such a magnificent temple have affected their relationship with God?

Though the present was bitter, the Jews in captivity had to admit they deserved the chastisement they had received. Plans for the temple in hand, Ezekiel could offer hope for God's people.

A Procedure for Worship

Ezekiel 43:13—46:24 gives dimensions for the altar of burnt offering. In addition, it explains the roles of the priests and the Prince during the Millennium. A detailed study of the section reveals many similarities to the system of worship that Moses established. However, several differences from the old system are obvious.

The presence of sacrifices during Christ's Kingdom is a great puzzle to some. Hasn't the sacrifice of Christ made other sacrifices unnecessary? If Christ's sacrifice took away people's sin, how can millennial sacrifices be appropriate?

These sacrifices are not a throwback to the old Levitical system. The Old Testament sacrifices both pictured Christ's death in advance and provided an atonement, or covering, for sins until Christ took away those sins by the sacrifice of Himself, once for all. The millennial sacrifices will picture Christ's death, serving only as memorials of His finished work, in much the same vein as our celebration of the Lord's Table.

12. Read 1 Corinthians 11:24–26. When we take Communion, or the Lord's Supper, we do it for a specific reason; what is that reason?

13. Read Hebrews 10:4. What did Old Testament animal sacrifices fail to do?

The sacrifices of the Levitical system, when made with faith, covered sin and restored the believer to fellowship with God. Old Testament saints were saved by grace through faith, just as New Testament saints are. The blood of Christ has always been the only means to Heaven (Romans 3:25, 26).

We may wonder, Why go back to the Mosaic system? However, millennial worship, including sacrifices, is not a return to the Mosaic system. After God deals with Israel's sin and imparts new life to the people (Ezekiel 37), the law can be used for its original purpose. God's people will enjoy fellowship with Him.

Ezekiel's record shows other differences from the system of worship that Moses established. In the system of the law, the high priest went into the Holy of Holies to intercede for the people. He sprinkled atoning blood on the mercy seat for the willful sins of the nation. He represented them before God.

14. Read Hebrews 3:1; 6:20; 10:10. Who performed the same task, "once for all" and is the Great High Priest?

15. Why won't a high priest be needed in the Millennium?

16. Read Ezekiel 45:21–25; Leviticus 23:34. What two feasts will be observed in the Millennium?

The Passover reminded Israel of God's great redemption from slavery in Egypt. During the Millennium, this feast will have new significance. As the people celebrate in the Kingdom, the Lamb of God Who takes away the sin of the world will be present as King. The people will celebrate God's deliverance in full.

The people will also celebrate the Feast of Tabernacles. For seven days a year, Old Testament Israelites camped out in booths that they had made (Leviticus 23:33–44). This annual reminder of the forty years of wilderness wanderings helped Israel remember God's faithfulness. He had led them through the wilderness into the Promised Land. As Israel celebrates the Feast of Tabernacles in the Kingdom, it will have an even deeper significance. Israel had sinned against the Lord and received discipline from Him. He kept His promise to bring her back and establish His Kingdom in her. He brought her to life and under the rule of Messiah. God brought Israel to the fulfillment of His Word.

Restored Land

17. Ezekiel 47:1–12. What miraculous and abundant things will occur in the Millennium?

The millennial temple will be the source of a river. This river will produce life and healing (47:9). The magnitude of the river will generate hope. The messenger took Ezekiel out 4,000 cubits into the water until the current made further progress impossible. This source of life will be abundant!

The boundaries of millennial Israel will approximate those specified by Moses (Numbers 34:3–12). The Lord, Who always keeps His Word, promised the land to Israel's forefathers (Ezekiel 47:14). Each of the tribes will have an equal share of land. Boundaries will run in straight east-west lines, all across the land. As Jacob specified, Manasseh and Ephraim, the two sons of Joseph, will each receive a portion of the inheritance (48:4, 5).

The center of the land will be allotted to the priests, the Levites, and the Prince (vv. 8–22). Its pastureland and farmland will supply the needs of those who serve the Lord in the temple and the city. Jerusalem, destroyed for the sins of the nation, will be restored. In its new form, it will have twelve gates, named for the sons of Jacob (vv. 31–34).

Restored Fellowship

Ezekiel 48:35b gives a great gift to Jerusalem. The city's name is changed. In the Old Testament, a name was linked to one's character or reputation. The Lord had made Jerusalem a reproach and laughingstock among the nations. In that day He will give the city a new name, signifying her new reputation.

18. Ezekiel 48:35. What will Jerusalem's new name be?

Israel's new name will mean that God is present in her. The most important characterization of Jerusalem will be the abiding presence of God. Israel will never be disciplined by the Lord again. He will dwell with His people forever. Never again will they be tempted to turn to lifeless idols, for God will be present with them. He will fulfill every word of His promises. God's glory will abide with God's people!

19. How is Ezekiel 48:35 a "happily ever after" for Israel?

Believers are in the presence of God right now through the indwelling of the Holy Spirit.

20. How should God's presence in us impact our lives?

21. How will His presence be different and affect us when we are in Heaven for eternity?

22. How should this truth influence us now?

Making It Personal

23. What did you learn from the study of Ezekiel that has changed the way you view your own sin?

24. What are some steps you will take as a result of this study to stay in fellowship with God?

25. The book of Ezekiel is about sin, judgment, holiness, and restoration. How committed are you to forsaking sin, avoiding judgment, being holy, and keeping in fellowship with God?

        __ uncommitted

        __ slightly committed

        __ deeply committed

26. Memorize Ezekiel 48:35b.